MANAGING BUSINESS RESOURCES

For CCEA AS Unit 2

Ian Bickerstaff

Rewarding Learning

Colourpoint
Educational

© Ian Bickerstaff and Colourpoint Books 2008

ISBN: 978 1 906578 02 2

First Edition
Third Impression, 2014

Layout and design: April Sky Design
Printed by: W&G Baird Ltd, Antrim

The Author

Ian Bickerstaff is an experienced examiner, having acted as an assistant examiner for GCE Economics, and currently a principal examiner of both GCE Business Studies and GCE Applied Business. He is also a principal moderator of the Wider Key Skills. Ian has a combined Honours degree in Economics and Education and a Master's degree in Business Administration (MBA). He is employed as a university lecturer, teaching Accounting, Strategic Issues and Entrepreneurship. He is curently researching Entrepreneurship Education.

Ian is also the author of the popular text for GCE Applied Business entitled *Finance,* also published by Colourpoint.

Acknowledgements

Thanks must go to a number of people without whose help this book would not have been completed.

Firstly, to my wife Gail and my son Ryan for their unending patience and support; to my mother and father for their encouragement throughout the years; and Una McCann at Colourpoint for her words of advice and encouragement.

COLOURPOINT
EDUCATIONAL

Colourpoint Educational
An imprint of Colourpoint Creative Ltd
Colourpoint House
Jubilee Business Park
21 Jubilee Road
Newtownards
County Down
Northern Ireland
BT23 4YH

Tel: 028 9182 6339
Fax: 028 9182 1900
E-mail: info@colourpoint.co.uk
Web site: www.colourpoint.co.uk

Picture credits

Colourpoint: 93

IStockphoto: 8, 11, 14, 16, 17, 18, 20, 22, 24, 26, 28, 33, 34, 35, 37, 38, 44, 50, 52, 54, 56, 61, 63, 66, 70, 79, 81, 82, 91, 96, 97

Malcolm Johnston: 45, 91

Shelia Johnston: 17

US Federal Government: 47

CONTENTS

This text covers AS Unit 2 (Managing Business Resources) of the CCEA Specification for GCE Business Studies.

Chapter 1: ORGANISATIONAL DESIGN

There are different types of business organisation, including sole traders, partnerships and companies. Each of these types of organisations will have similar financial and legal structures but the way that each is organised internally will be different. Each business organisation will have its own internal structure. This is known as the business' Formal Organisation Structure.

These will be different because the internal operations and dynamics will be unique to each individual business. The way that a business is structured will be determined by many different factors, some of which may be:

- The relationships between individuals
- Who is in charge
- Who has authority to make decisions
- Who carries out decisions
- How information is communicated

Although each organisation will have its own structure, there are often similarities between businesses. For example, most businesses are organised into departments who have departmental heads, who are in charge of a number of employees.

Some organisations are structured as a result of natural development that arises as a result of the employees who are employed in the organisation. Against this, organisations may create a structure which identifies all of the necessary jobs that are required. Employees are then appointed to fill these positions.

Irrespective of how the organisation developed, and as a result of change in the firm's external environment, the organisational structure will also change and may result in the necessity to restructure.

It is possible to identify a common set of features that organisational design should try to achieve.

- The chosen organisation design should group its activities into different departments such as production, finance, and sales
- The organisation design should show clearly the relationships between employees
- The organisational design should show the channels of communication for the organisation
- The division of work among employees should be evident

ORGANISATION CHARTS

Many firms produce organisation charts which illustrate the structure of the organisation. These are useful for many reasons.

- They can highlight any potential communication problems because the chart shows how employees are linked to each other. If there is a breakdown in communication, the chart can be used to identify where this has occurred.
- Organisation charts allow individuals to see where they fit into the overall structure of the organisation and who they are responsible to and what they are responsible for.
- Organisation charts allow firms to identify where specialist members of staff are required.
- Organisation charts show how different departments relate to each other.

Although organisation charts are useful in that they show an overall picture of the organisation, they can also have some drawbacks. Employees may feel demotivated if they feel that they have not been given the correct status on the chart. Additionally, if they appear near the bottom of the chart, this could add to their discontent.

TASK

Evaluate the advantages and disadvantages of having an organisation chart in the following organisations:

a)   A small corner shop

b)   A farm run by three brothers

c)   A retail outlet with eight branches throughout the country

d)   A multinational manufacturing organisation

THE HIERARCHY

When designing the organisation structure for a business, one factor that needs to be considered is the hierarchy. This refers to the order or levels of management in a firm and the chain of command. Businesses must consider the number of levels in the chain of command and decide on the most appropriate for the organisation.

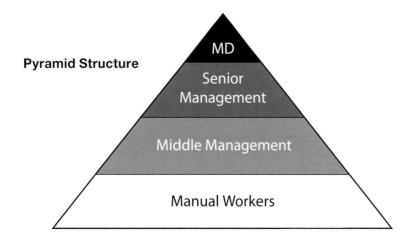

Pyramid Structure

MD
Senior Management
Middle Management
Manual Workers

ORGANISATIONAL DESIGN

THE SPAN OF CONTROL

Another factor to consider is the span of control, which is the number of subordinates working under one superior. If a superior has eight people working under him/her, the span of control is eight. A narrow span of control (few subordinates) ensures that a superior has tight control over subordinates and can supervise them easily. Better and quicker communication is also possible and it allows better coordination between subordinates to take place. The major drawbacks of a narrow span of control are that subordinates may not be motivated because they have little freedom. From an organisational perspective, a narrow span of control has the disadvantage of being costly; more superiors are required to oversee a small number of employees.

A narrow span of control

A wide span of control requires superiors to delegate more work and allows subordinates to have more freedom as they are less closely supervised. However, the major drawback of a wide span of control is that it requires a suitable superior who has the capability of managing a large number of people.

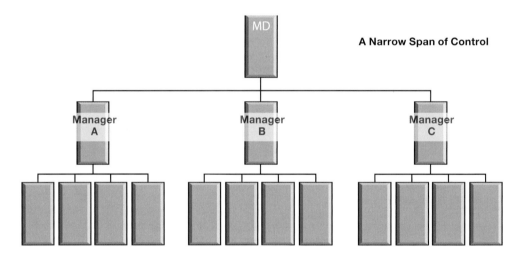

A Narrow Span of Control

A wide span of control

There are various ideas as to what makes a suitable span of control but it is very much dependent on the organisation itself. The following must be taken into account:

- The nature of the task. If the work is repetitive, it is easier to supervise a larger number of subordinates.
- The group of subordinates. If the workers naturally gel, it will allow a larger span of control.
- The ability and experience of superiors and subordinates.
- Communications. If there is a good communication system in place, this will facilitate a wider span of control.

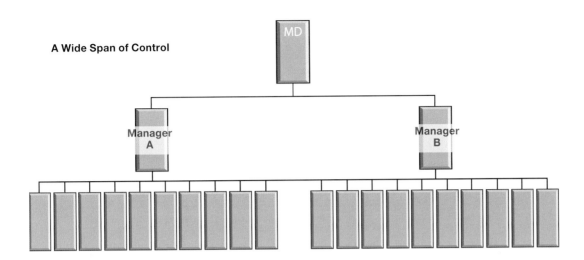

A Wide Span of Control

FLAT AND TALL ORGANISATIONS

The span of control chosen for an organisation will have consequences for the 'height' of an organisation. An organisation with a narrow span of control will have an organisation structure which is tall, whereas one with a wide span of control will be flatter.

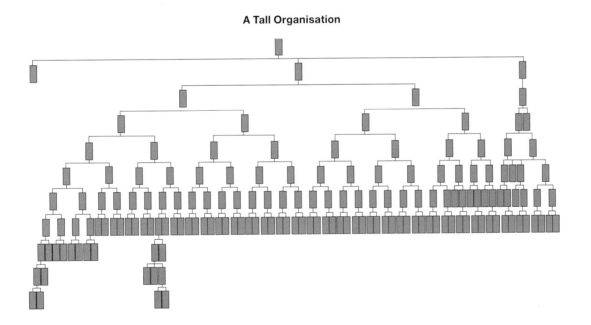

A Tall Organisation

A Flat Organisation

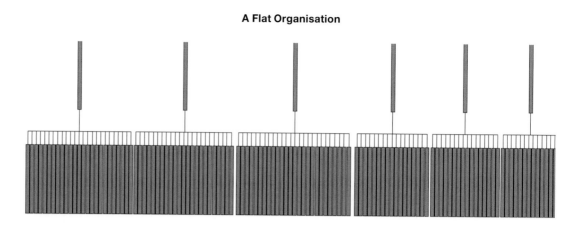

DELAYERING

In recent times there has been a tendency to remove layers within organisations and create flatter organisations. This practice removes management layers in an attempt to make the organisation more efficient. Communication and decision-making is speeded up, although it may be argued that the managers who are left simply have more to do. Unless these managers have the correct skills and the capability to 'manage' more, the advantages that should be gained can be lost.

TASK

Discuss, using examples, the appropriateness of different organisational structures to a business.

CASE STUDY

MARKS AND SPENCER

Marks and Spencer employs more than 60,000 employees with around 3,000 employed in its Head Office in London. These head office employees perform a variety of roles, ranging from accountancy and marketing, to purchasing and the management of stocks. Throughout the organisation, management have the task of leading, training and motivating people, not only in the United Kingdom but throughout their franchise outlets overseas.

Marks and Spencer decided to change their organisation structure from a tall structure to a newer flatter structure. They achieved this through a process of delayering which gave employees throughout the organisation more accountability than they had before. This means that employees now have to explain and justify any decisions that they make.

CASE STUDY...

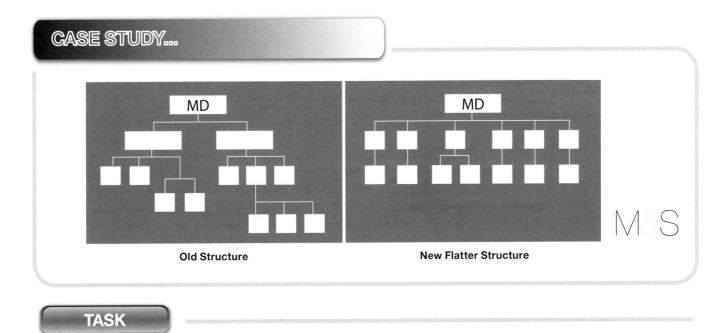

| Old Structure | New Flatter Structure |

TASK

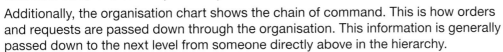

Evaluate the implications of Marks and Spencer moving to a new organisation structure.

AUTHORITY AND RESPONSIBILITY

On an organisation chart, employees who appear at higher levels have more authority and more responsibility than those who appear at lower levels on the chart. Conversely, employees at lower levels have less authority and less responsibility. The major difference between these two areas is that authority may be passed down to someone else, whereas responsibility cannot.

Additionally, the organisation chart shows the chain of command. This is how orders and requests are passed down through the organisation. This information is generally passed down to the next level from someone directly above in the hierarchy.

ORGANISATIONAL FUNCTIONS

Most firms which produce and sell products or services will organise themselves using six key functional areas. Firms which are not involved in production may still organise themselves using some of these areas:

- Production
- Finance
- Human Resources
- Sales and Marketing
- Administration
- Research and Development

Each of these functional areas needs to work together so that the whole organisation has the same aims and objectives. This will require good communication throughout the organisation.

One way of achieving this is to develop a clear set of company objectives and ensure that each functional area is aware of them. These objectives then need to be further broken down into specific objectives for each function.

We shall now examine the roles and tasks performed by each of these functional areas.

ORGANISATIONAL DESIGN

Production Function

The production section of the organisation is responsible for turning raw materials (inputs) into finished products (outputs). This section must ensure that this process is carried out efficently.

A key aspect of modern production is ensuring an acceptable level of quality in the finished product.

Finance function

The finance section of the organisation keeps records of money received and paid out. This information is used to produce various financial statements and is also used to produce management accounts for senior managers. This will allow them to plan and review business strategy.

The finance section may also be responsible for administering employee expenses and salaries.

Human resources function

The human resources section has responsibility for the recruitment, selection, training and development of staff. The purpose of this is to develop staff so that they contribute to achieving the organisation's objectives.

This resource sector often adopts a welfare role for employees and may also create policies that balance organisational needs with those of the employee. They will also ensure that the organisation is complying with employee legislation.

Sales and marketing function

The marketing section will research customer needs. It will investigate which market the organisation is aiming at, the type of consumer making up the market (age, sex etc) and the preferences of the consumer within that market. This information will then be used to produce a product that meets consumer needs. Once the product has been designed by the production department, marketing will then need to package, advertise, and promote the product.

The sales section is responsible for persuading the consumer to purchase the organisation's product.

Administrative function

The administrative section deals with all administrative tasks, producing documents (eg forms, stationery) for the organisation, and maintaining the organisation's premises and equipment.

This function, although not always recognised, is vital, as it holds the organisation together. Without an administrative department, customer complaints would not be resolved, customer orders may not be processed, and the workforce may not have the tools they need to complete their tasks.

Research and development function

The research and development section aims to improve existing products, create new and better products, improve production methods, and create effective processes. This will enable the organisation to reduce costs, increase profitability and remain ahead of the competition.

ADVANTAGES AND DISADVANTAGES OF A FUNCTIONAL STRUCTURE

Functional structure

Advantages

- *Specialisation.* Each department focuses on its own work. This allows workers to concentrate on what they are good at which should result in efficiency for the organisation.
- *Accountability.* A functional organisation structure will help to identify exactly where different processes take place. This means it is easy to identify who is responsible for the different activities in the organisation.
- *Clarity.* The organisation chart will help employees to clarify exactly what their role is, as well as the role of others.

Disadvantages

- **Resistance to change.** Individual functional areas can become resistant to change as they tend to concentrate on their own section's activities. Therefore, the overall objectives of the organisation can sometimes conflict with individual functional objectives.
- **Coordination.** Each functional area concentrates on its own specific tasks which can result in poor coordination between the different functional areas. For example, there may be conflict between sales and production whereby sales are trying to maximise the quantities of goods sold but the production function may not be able to keep up with this.
- **Gap between top and bottom.** Functional structures can have a long chain of command which can result in slow decision-making and remoteness between employees at different levels of the hierarchy.

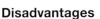

TASK

> Explain why many organisations need to structure themselves into different functional areas.

ALTERNATIVE WAYS TO STRUCTURE A BUSINESS

So far we have assumed that organisations structure themselves by function. Although this is a relatively common method of structuring, there are other alternatives that may be considered.

- **By product:** organising the business according to the different products made or activity carried out.
- **By area:** organising the business according to geographical or regional structure.
- **By customer:** organising the business according to different customer needs.
- **By process:** organising the business according to the stages that a product goes through when being made.
- **Matrix:** An organisation structured this way contains teams of people created from various sections of the business.

ADVANTAGES AND DISADVANTAGES OF ALTERNATIVE WAYS TO STRUCTURE A BUSINESS

ORGANISATION BY PRODUCT

Advantages

- **Clear focus.** A clear focus on the market segment helps to meet customers' needs. If those involved in, for example, production are constantly producing the same product then they will become specialists in this product and will be able to react to changes in consumer needs. This may not be possible if a production team are producing a wide range of products.

- **Competition.** Positive competition between divisions may take where teams responsible for different products may try to out-perform each other. This will not only take place in production but will occur in other areas such as sales and marketing.
- **Better control.** Each division can act as a separate profit centre which means that it is easier to assess the performance of individual products. In a functional structure, this is not as easy as products are grouped together within the different functional areas.

Disadvantages

- **Duplication of functions.** A major disadvantage of organisation by product is the duplication that takes place. As each division is responsible for all of the activities associated with their individual product, there will be situations where extra staff may be required. For example, a different sales force may be required for each division.
- **Negative effects of competition.** It may be argued that competition within an organisation is not always good. The competition may encourage disharmony in the workplace as individuals compete against each other, and there is the danger that shortcuts may be taken.
- **Lack of central control.** Another major drawback with this structure is that there will be a lack of central control over each separate division. This arises because each division has control over its own product.

ORGANISATION BY AREA

Advantages

- **Serve local needs better.** Individual parts of the organisation will be located close to the customer which means that local and individual needs can be met.
- **Positive competition.** As each unit will be on its own, competition between different geographical units may take place. This may result in increased efficiency.
- **More effective communication between the business and local customers.** The organisation will be in a better position to understand these needs as they are located near the customers.

Disadvantages

- **Conflict between local and central management.** Conflict can arise because on one hand each unit is self-sufficient and seeking to meet individual needs, but at the same time they are still responsible to central management.
- **Duplication of resources and functions.** As each unit is self-sufficient, there will be a duplication of resources. For example, machinery will be required at each individual unit, a separate sales team will be required etc.

BY CUSTOMER

Advantages

- This may be appropriate in situations where customers are offered different facilities, by various departments that specialise for their needs.

Disadvantages

- This structure can be very costly as it requires almost one-to-one treatment of customers.

BY PROCESS

This structure may be appropriate in situations where a series of processes are performed to produce a product.

Advantages

- This structure allows management to identify clearly where problems are arising in the production process.
- It allows new technology to be introduced at any stage of production.

Disadvantages

- A major problem with this structure is that duplication can occur if different people are involved in similar processes across a range of products.

MATRIX ORGANISATIONS

A Matrix structure organisation contains teams of people created from various sections of the business and it is led by a project manager. The teams are created for the purposes of a specific project and will often only exist for the duration of the project. They are usually deployed to develop new products and services.

Advantages

- Individuals can be chosen according to the needs of the project.
- The use of a project team, which is dynamic and specialised, can view problems in a different way.
- Project managers are directly responsible for completing the project within a specific deadline and budget.

Disadvantages

- A conflict of loyalty can develop between line managers and project managers over the allocation of resources.
- If teams have a lot of independence, they can be difficult to monitor.
- Costs can be increased if more project managers are created through the use of project teams.

QUESTIONS

Give examples of organisations that might use each of the above business structures.

Is it possible for organisations to adopt more than one business structure? What are the advantages and disadvantages of adopting such an approach?

CENTRALISATION AND DECENTRALISATION

Centralisation and decentralisation refer to how decisions are taken within an organisation. In a centralised organisation, most decisions are taken at the top tiers of the organisation. This means that subordinates have very little authority. A decentralised organisation on the other hand is one where subordinates do have authority to make decisions.

In deciding the degree of centralisation or decentralisation that will exist within an organisation, there is a range of factors that must be considered:

- **Cost.** If a decision is going to be costly for an organisation, it is likely that top management will want to make such decisions.
- **Uniformity.** If an organisation wants uniformity throughout its operations, it is likely that decision-making will be centralised.
- **Size.** If an organisation is very large, it may be difficult to centralise decision-making. Therefore decentralisation may not only be desirable but essential.
- **History.** Organisations which grow organically are often centralised because the original owners and the culture associated with the business are retained.
- **The quality of junior management.** Decentralisation requires top management providing juniors with authority. In order to capitalise on this, the junior managers need to be capable of assuming this authority.

Advantages of centralisation

- Senior management can retain control. This may be particularly important in areas such as finance.
- Economies of scale may be achieved in an organisation if everything is centralised.
- Conflict can sometimes arise between different departments or sections within an organisation. A centralised approach allows a balance to be achieved and can minimise such conflict.
- Decisions should be of a higher quality because they are being made by more experienced people.

Advantages of decentralisation

- Subordinates may be motivated as they have some authority over the decision-making process.
- The workload of senior management can be shared.
- Subordinates may be in a better position to make decisions because they are at the 'coal face'. Senior management may be too remote to make some decisions.
- Decision-making is accelerated and can be more flexible if decentralisation is evident.
- Junior management will gain experience of the decision-making process, which will provide a natural pool of workers to occupy the more senior positions in the future.

CASE STUDY

Decentralisation in Tesco

Tesco, the United Kingdom-based international supermarket chain, has its headquarters located in Cheshunt, England. The organisation is an example of a decentralised business because each store in the Tesco chain of supermarkets has its own store manager who makes the decisions concerning the store he or she is managing. All the store managers in a region report to the regional manager.

Power in Tesco is passed 'down the line' and people at the lower end of the scale of power can make decisions about what happens within their store.

Tesco provide the framework for pricing, layout, staff terms etc, but individual managers can operate flexibly to a certain degree within that structure.

Supporters of this type of structure feel that this enables people who are close to the shop floor to make decisions best suited to the customer.

TASK

Evaluate the advantages and disadvantages of Tesco adopting a decentralised organisation structure.

CASE STUDY

Weldit is a specialised engineering company which was formed by Mark Fletcher in 1975. Mark had a hands-on approach to running the organisation. Thus, tight managerial supervision, a small degree of delegation of authority, and a highly personalised form of management had accounted for its success in the early years.

However, in recent times, changes in technology have greatly affected the organisation, and the company had been losing much of its market share.

In view of this situation, the board of directors, at a recent general meeting, agreed to call in a team of management consultants to evaluate the organisation structure and the management practices of the company.

The consultants spent five months gathering and analysing facts about the company. They interviewed employees, reviewed company reports, and visited numerous offices and sites. They soon became aware of Mark's influence on the company's operations. His management style and beliefs were evident throughout the company. Although the company had grown and prospered, the consultants were surprised to find that it had done so despite the fact that certain principles of organisational design were, in their opinion, ignored.

The consultants found, for example, that the company had never had an organisation chart. Nowhere in the information collected by the consultants could they find documents which defined the duties

CASE STUDY...

and responsibilities of managers. Job descriptions were not used and there was no evidence of formal job titles. According to those who were interviewed, Mark believed that formalising the organisation would result in loss of initiative because people would begin to feel restricted.

They would act on problems only if they were clearly within their remit. He stressed that co-operation could achieve coordination.

Consistent with the absence of organisation charts, there was also little use of other means to recognise authority. No names or titles appeared on doors or correspondence. Each senior member of staff was expected to know who did what in the company. There was no formal hierarchy of positions; each manager was considered equal, although some could take control of dealing with a problem for which he had special competence. 'The best man for the job at the time' was a phrase used throughout the company.

One consequence of Mark's management style was that his span of control consisted of some 15 line managers. In addition, another 15 staff members reported to him. The number of managerial levels was minimal in comparison to other similar organisations.

The consultants were particularly surprised to find such a wide span at the top of the organisation. They also discovered that employees down the line received direction from numerous managers, including Mark himself. This practice undermined the authority of intermediate managers, and caused confusion as to who subordinates were accountable.

The consultants were convinced that the company should attempt to develop a more formal structure. Mark may have been correct in thinking that undefined jobs, ambiguously delegated authority, and wide spans of control were appropriate during the early days of the company's growth, but that time had passed. The consultants recommended that Mark should begin immediately to formalise the structure of the organisation.

1. Explain why the organisation flourished in its early days despite having no formal organisation structure.

2. What factors should Mark consider when formalising the company's organisation structure?

CCEA SPECIMEN QUESTION - SUMMER 06 A2 1

Read the information below and answer the questions that follow.

Organisation Structure and Motivation

Nicola Winters is the Managing Director of Audimus Ltd. The company produces expensive, high quality radios, mainly for the UK market. Audimus Ltd is a family owned business and a large proportion of its workforce has been with the firm for more than 10 years. Many of its working practices have been left unchanged as it has expanded rapidly over the last few years.

Nicola now wants to introduce two important changes within the production department. Firstly, she has become aware that each assembly line supervisor has a relatively narrow span of control compared to that within more modernised factories. While this was once justified as being necessary to achieve high quality in production, Nicola realises that it is too costly and that each supervisor's

CCEA SPECIMEN QUESTIONS...

span of control must be significantly increased. This idea has not gone down well with the supervisors who are concerned about health and safety issues.

In addition, the assembly line workers are currently paid on an hourly basis. Nicola wants Audimus Ltd to change to a payments by results (PBR) system, such as piece-rate, with workers being offered bonuses for achieving productivity targets. She is convinced that this would make the company more competitive in the future.

(a) Explain what is meant by the term 'narrow span of control'. [4]

(b) Discuss the factors that might influence the span of control of the assembly line supervisors within Audimus Ltd. [8]

Chapter 2: COMMUNICATION

2

Good communication is necessary for the efficient running of any business. Communication takes place at all levels within an organisation and will only be effective if it is received and understood.

METHODS OF COMMUNICATION

There are many different ways of communicating and the chosen method will depend on many factors. Communication may be classified using the following categories:

- Verbal
- Non-Verbal
- Written
- Numerical
- Technological

Verbal

This method of communication has the advantage of being quick and flexible as it can be adjusted to the given circumstances. Moreover, it can be effected cheaply and misunderstandings can be clarified immediately. This method of communication can be supported by non-verbal methods of communication such as the use of body language. This can help to reinforce verbal communication.

There are however some drawbacks with verbal communication – the main one being its lack of permanence as it is not written down. There can also be problems with misunderstandings that may arise as a result of the way that words are spoken. The same combination of words for example, could be communicated as a request or as an order, depending on the tone used by the communicator. This may cause problems for recipients, especially those who do not speak English as their first language. Furthermore, statements can be made which are later regretted.

Non-verbal

Non-Verbal communication is useful for communicating very simple messages such as pleasure or criticism. This form of communication can take many forms such as the use of expressions or gestures. In many instances a face to face meeting might be more appropriate than a telephone conversation if these forms of non-verbal communication need to be emphasised.

Written

The main advantage of using written communication is that the message can be presented precisely and will be permanent. Greater thought can be put into the message and receivers can read the message at their own speed. It is however a time-consuming form of communication and can completely fail to meet its objectives if it is not read. Additionally, written messages can be misinterpreted if the sender is not present.

Numerical

This form of communication involves the use of tables, statistics and graphs. It is often used as a way of providing a more complete message than words, and can have a great impact. Because the information is presented pictorially, it can help the receiver to understand figures and statistics. Nonetheless, it is difficult to use on its own, as misunderstandings can arise if it is not supported by a commentary.

Technological communication

This form of communication may involve the use of computers or other machinery such as facsimile (fax) machines and mobile phones. Although this may be an expensive form of communication in terms of initial investment, technological communication can be very cost effective. It is also fast and is usually of a high quality.

THE COMMUNICATION PROCESS

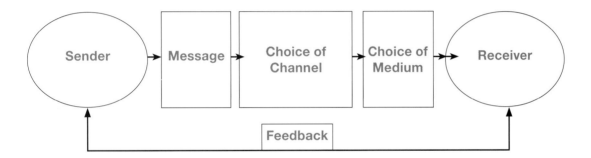

For successful communication to take place, it is important that the information being sent is fully understood by both the sender and the receiver. This will help to determine the choice of communication channel and the medium used to send the message.

COMMUNICATION CHANNEL

Communication can take place using a variety of communication channels.

Downward (vertical) communication is normally used to tell employees about decisions that have already been made.

Upward (vertical) communication helps managers to understand employees' views and concerns. It is also a good mechanism for receiving feedback, and it can help workers feel involved in the organisation, and thereby improve motivation.

Horizontal communication takes place between people at the same level within an organisation.

Diagonal communication exists where communication takes place between people at different levels in the organisation.

Analyse the impact of technology on communication channels.

FORMAL/INFORMAL COMMUNICATION

Within all businesses there are both formal and informal channels of communication. Formal channels are those that have been approved by employers and employee

representatives. Informal communication (often referred to as the grapevine) can be both helpful and a hindrance to the formal communication process; because the channel is not an approved one, management has no control over it. This means that communications can become distorted and can be taken out of context. An example of the dangers of informal communication can be illustrated by the children's game 'Chinese Whispers'. Despite these limitations, management recognises the benefits that can arise from using the grapevine. Information may be 'leaked' by management to see what the reaction might be within the organisation. Research would suggest that effective communication within an organisation requires both formal and informal communication.

TASK

Describe the differences between internal and external communications and formal and informal communications.

MEDIUM OF COMMUNICATION

As already discussed, information can be conveyed using a variety of media ranging from written methods to oral methods. Some examples of communication mediums include the following:

Oral

- Meetings
- Conferences
- Training Courses
- Consultations
- Telephone
- Presentations

Written

- Memos
- Reports
- Agendas
- Minutes
- Notices
- Letters
- Shareholder Reports

Numerical

- Posters
- Wall Charts
- Graphs

Technological

- Internet
- Facsimile Machines (Fax)
- Mobile Phones (Texting)
- E-Mail

CASE STUDY

PENSIONS FEARS EASED BY COMMUNICATIONS BLITZ AT MARKET RESEARCH FIRM

Two-thirds of workers at market research firm Information Resources are confident of earning their target retirement income after the company carried out a communications blitz.

The firm scrapped its online financial benefits site and brought in a more personalised approach in a bid to improve retention.

Managing director for Northern Europe, Jeremy McNamara, wrote to every member of staff explaining the changes and encouraging staff to plan for their retirement. Every individual was then encouraged to attend an individual meeting with a financial adviser, organised by the company.

More than 90% of employees responded to the initiative, with half saying it would influence any decision to stay at Information Resources, and 65% saying they would now be able to meet their financial retirement goals. HR director Ros Smith said: "Since we implemented the improvements, our employees have an increased awareness of their financial and retirement options. The personalised, face-to-face strategy proved to be very effective in communicating the benefits and offering advice to each individual employee."

Source: www.PersonnelToday.com 26 June 2008

TASK

Explain why you think the use of a face-to-face strategy was effective in his situation.

CASE STUDY

RESEARCH REVEALS THE UK WORKFORCE'S INCREASING DEPENDENCY ON E-MAIL AND ELECTRONIC COMMUNICATION

New research has revealed an increasing dependency on e-mail and electronic communication as a vital means of keeping in touch with the office.

A survey conducted by ICM Research for software provider Nasstar, found that half of 25 to 34 year olds said they could not function without access to e-mail.

CASE STUDY...

This figure dropped to four in 10 teenagers admitting their reliance on e-mail, but increased to 44% among 35 to 44 year-olds.

The survey revealed that 43% of respondents in the South East said they would struggle without e-mail access, against only one-third of respondents in Wales and the South West.

Four in 10 women admitted they would find life difficult without e-mail contact, compared to 38% of men.

Charles Black, chief executive of Nasstar, said: "Thirty and 40-somethings have fitted e-mail into their busy lives as a vital form of communication. It's not restricted by time; you can e-mail in the middle of the night without disturbing anyone. And now it's no longer restricted by location.

"While teenagers are passionate about their mobile phones and texting in particular, the older generations are relying more and more on e-mail because of its use in a business capacity. E-mail really works for business people on the go," Black said.

Source: www.PersonnelToday.com 19 June 2007

TASK

Evaluate the pros and cons of this increased dependency on e-mail and electronic communication.

ACTIVITY

Write a brief note explaining what each of the above communications media are, giving an example of when they would be appropriate to use.

FACTORS AFFECTING CHOICE OF MEDIUM

There is a range if factors affecting choice of medium, some of which are lised below:

- **Direction of Communication.** The nature of the message might dictate the medium that is available for communication. For example, posters are only suitable for downward communications.
- **Nature of the communication.** If a communication is confidential, it is important to choose an appropriate medium of communication.
- **Costs.** It is important that the message is conveyed using the most cost effective means.
- **Speed.** How quickly a message needs to be communicated will play a major part in selecting the most appropriate medium.
- **Length of message.** Verbal communication may not be appropriate if a message is long.

BARRIERS TO COMMUNICATION

The model on page 21 illustrating the communication process, shows that communication will only be effective if the message is received and understood by the receiver. However, there are a number of factors that might prevent this from happening.

- Sometimes a message can contain too much jargon or technical information. The receiver may be confused if they are not sure what the information means.
- It is essential that the sender does not make too many assumptions about the ability of the receiver to understand the message being sent, or underestimates the scope for 'reading into' the message things that are not there.
- A message can become unclear if there is too much information included in it.
- If a receiver is not prepared to listen to the message, this can cause a breakdown in the communication process.
- If a message has to travel through a long line of different people, this can lead to the message becoming lost or distorted.
- The wrong choice of communication channel can result in ineffective communications.
- Sometimes the wrong information is sent to the wrong person.

ACTIVITY

From the following list of situations, suggest an appropriate medium and method of communication that should be used. Identify who should be part of the communication process and highlight any problems that might arise if the communication is handled incorrectly.

a) Notice that 30 members out of a staff of 100 are facing redundancy
b) A minute's silence at the firm to be held in memory of a worker who has died suddenly
c) Notification of the intention to increase staff pay
d) An announcement that a staff member is expecting her first baby
e) Plans to expand operations and relocate part of the factory to Asia
f) Congratulations to a member of staff who has raised £1,000 for charity by completing a marathon
g) Notification that, due to maintenance, computer networks will be closed down for 24 hours
h) An announcement that a member of staff is retiring after a long and distinguished career
i) An announcement that company profits have increased by 25%
j) The introduction of a new photocopier that has many additional features
k) The successful completion of performance targets by members of staff
l) An urgent query about an order from a customer
m) Details of company performance during the previous six months

TASK

Evaluate the importance of efficient communication procedures for a large manufacturing organisation.

CASE STUDY

Communication break down

The fast-changing nature of today's business environment means it is crucial that the lines of communication between management and the shop-floor are effective, trusted and always open.

The business world is in the midst of a period of unprecedented turbulence. Once this would have been considered wholly negative, but today we are seeing a new model of uncertainty, which is as much about opportunities as threats.

Organisations are specialising, generalising, merging, acquiring, downsizing, expanding and restructuring at an alarming rate. Nothing is certain any more. Today's competitor is tomorrow's ally. The next development in technology could potentially wipe out a whole market overnight or give birth to a total new breed of business.

Add to this the aftermath of the terrorist attacks of 11 September and the threat of recession, and it's clear that if businesses are to survive and thrive in these challenging times, they need to become more agile and responsive.

Used strategically, communication is the cement that will bind the organisation together and ensure people's energies are focused in the right direction. But the mixture – and the application – needs to be right.

A new style of communication with employees must be developed – one that is less about directing and more about engaging with people. Yet many organisations are trapped in a time warp, using a style of communication that is more suited to the production lines of the 1970s than to the fast and flexible companies of today.

Businesses need to help employees find their way through the increasing mass of information heaped upon them so they can focus on what's really important. They must refine the way they use technology to communicate, to ensure the medium doesn't cloud the message. They have to find new ways of helping employees build relationships and share knowledge – often over distance, and with people they may never have met and will work with only for a short time.

Uncertainty is worse than bad news

How often does this happen in organisations? Change is coming, so senior managers spend hours locked in the boardroom refining their objectives, considering options and evaluating solutions. They then 'announce' their conclusions – and expect everyone to march meekly in the right direction.

The reality, however, is that in times of uncertainty, organisations need more than just compliance from employees. They need to engage people's hearts and minds, gain their energy and commitment and get them focusing their efforts in the right direction.

One of the first steps to doing this is to recognise the need to 'share the thinking'. In times of change, people are more stressed by uncertainty than by bad news. They are hungry for information about rationale, options, possible scenarios and implications. They also, naturally, want to know how it will affect them personally and what the organisation needs them to do differently in the new scenario.

Unfortunately, organisations in turmoil often want to keep their heads down and restrict

CASE STUDY

information. This may be because leaders are not clear themselves about what's going on, or what stance they should take, or because they are worried about disclosing confidential information. But even if you can't give people absolutes, you need at least to help them understand the context, appreciate how fast things are changing and give them a sense of the direction in which things might be heading.

If people understand the bigger organisational picture they will be more willing to stay for the ride and more motivated to do the job you need them to do. If they understand the specific role they need to play, they will be better equipped to make decisions and more willing to share knowledge and information with their colleagues.

If information is withheld, speculation and gossip will be rife and trust in management will be quickly eroded, at the very time you need everyone to be 'on side'. Equally, if employees only have half the picture, they may waste time and effort focusing their energies in completely the wrong direction.

Source: www.PersonnelToday.com 1 June 2002

Question
Analyse why workers at Sainsbury's may not find this approach motivational.

TASK

(a) Explain why effective communication is so important for organisations.

(b) Analyse any barriers to effective communication outlined in the case study.

Chapter 3: # MOTIVATION

3

It is important that individuals in the workplace are motivated. Although most people work to earn money, if they are happy in their workplace, they will put more effort into what they are doing and be more productive. This is clearly important to organisations since a productive workforce will improve efficiency and profitability.

If an organisation wants to motivate its employees, it needs to first identify what it is that motivates them and secondly seek ways to satisfy those needs. However, a further issue that organisations must consider is that all employees are different and so will be motivated by different things.

There is a range of factors that employees might consider to be important in a job:
- A good rate of pay
- Promotion prospects
- Good holidays
- Job security
- Good working relationships
- Responsibility
- Prestige

Although this list is not exhaustive, it is important to note that individual employees will place these motivators in differing orders of priority.

The desire to motivate employees has led to many different theories being developed. These attempt to provide an understanding of what motivates employees and make suggestions as to how better motivational systems can be implemented.

TAYLOR'S SCIENTIFIC MANAGEMENT

Frederick W Taylor set out a theory of Scientific Management in his book The Principles of Scientific Management in 1911. At this time production techniques and practices were very different to what they are today. Workers often brought their own tools to the workplace and decisions about the speed of machine operations were generally left to the operators. Workers rarely received training and they often restricted output because they feared that they would do themselves out of a job.

Taylor was critical about these practices, which led him to propose a scientific approach to managing the workforce. His belief was that efficiency would be achieved because the adopted methods were based on 'science'.

Some of his suggestions as to how to manage workers included the following principles:

- **Division of Labour.** Taylor believed that greater efficiency could be obtained in the workplace if workers specialised in those tasks that they were best at. Rather than workers being involved in the entire production of products, he suggested that the production process should be split up into different tasks. Individual employees would then be assigned to tasks that they were best at.

- **Managerial control over the workplace.** Management should have full control over areas such as the selection and training of workers as well as devising the best way to do things. Workers should also be supervised throughout the production process.

- **Measurement.** Individual aspects of the work process should be measurable and workers should be rewarded with an appropriate rate of pay to reflect their achievements. This involved the use of piece rates where employees would be paid according to how many 'pieces' they produced.

- **Standardisation, Efficiency and Discipline.** Work processes would be chosen according to how they could best be performed. This could involve the timing of individual tasks and the elimination of parts of the process that did not add anything to the completed task. Workers would then be taught these methods and would not be allowed to deviate from the sequence established.

Criticisms of Taylor

The major criticism of Taylor's approach was that he believed that workers were only interested in money and that they could be programmed like machines. He also assumed that there was one best way of doing things. Although this may be true for some employees, the best way was not necessarily the best way for everyone.

Taylor's approach is sometimes criticised in that it does not take into account the welfare of workers. Taylor would dispute this; he hoped that both management and workers would work in harmony as the methods adopted were based on scientific principles. If, by adopting these principles, workers performed well, ie greater levels of pieces produced, then this would be rewarded by increased wages.

TASK

Evaluate a firm's decision to adopt Taylor's Scientific management approach to employee motivation.

MASLOW'S HIERARCHY OF NEEDS

The first and perhaps the most famous motivational theory was developed by Abraham Maslow in 1954. Maslow felt that an employee's individual needs could be classified as either primary needs or secondary needs. He suggested that the needs of employees could be placed in a hierarchy where individual needs could be classified according to certain parameters. He argued that once a lower level need was met, an employee may move on to the next need in the hierarchy. These needs were categorised into five classes:

- Physiological needs
- Safety needs
- Love and belonging
- Esteem needs
- Self-actualisation

MOTIVATION

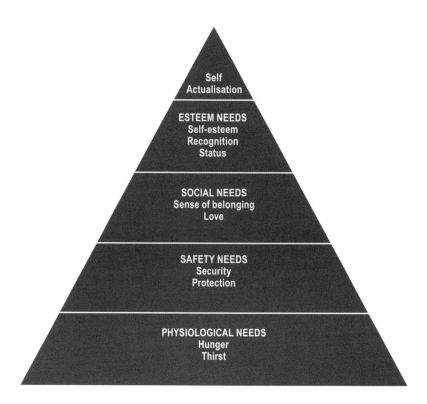

Physiological needs

These needs include obtaining food, drink and air. These are the strongest needs because they are necessary for physical survival and so must be satisfied. From an organisational perspective, paying an employee enough money to meet weekly bills can satisfy these needs.

Safety needs

When all physiological needs are satisfied, an individual's need for security can become active. Safety needs include the need to be protected from dangerous situations and from physical and psychological threats. Job security and a company pension scheme can help to satisfy these needs.

Needs of love, affection and belonging

When the needs for safety and for physiological well-being are satisfied, the next class of needs for love, affection and belonging may emerge. An organisation can seek to fulfil these needs by creating a working environment that allows employees to work with colleagues who support each other. Leisure facilities and sporting clubs can also help to fulfil these needs.

Needs for esteem

When the first three classes of needs are satisfied, the needs for esteem can arise. These involve needs for both self-esteem and for the esteem a person gains from others. When these needs are satisfied, the person feels self-confident and valuable as a person in the world. When these needs are not met, the person feels inferior, weak, helpless and worthless. An organisation can try to meet these needs by giving recognition for doing a job well. There are many ways that this may be done, such as reward schemes – employee of the month or incentive schemes.

Needs for self-actualisation

When all of the foregoing needs are satisfied, then and only then, are the needs for self-actualisation activated. Maslow describes self-actualisation as a person's need to be and do that which the person was "born to do". Therefore, self-actualisation will arise when a person needs to realise their full potential. These needs can be met if an organisation promotes an employee or gives them more responsibility. Although everyone is capable of fulfilling this need, Maslow argued that very few people actually reach this level.

Maslow's Hierarchy of Needs makes two important claims about the motivation of individuals. First, it is important to satisfy lower level needs before attempting to satisfy needs further up the hierarchy. Secondly, once a need is satisfied it will no longer motivate an individual.

Maslow's theory appears to have an important role in organisations. If management wants to motivate an individual, it should find out where the individual is on the hierarchy, ie which level, and then decide on ways of motivating that person. However, in practice, there can be some confusion and overlap as to where individuals might appear on the hierarchy. For example, money can fulfil physiological as well those needs linked to esteem.

TASK

Evaluate a firm's decision to adopt Maslow's approach to employee motivation.

DOUGLAS MCGREGOR

In 1960 Douglas McGregor published The Human Side of Enterprise which suggested that it is possible to categorise the reasons why people work and their attitude to responsibility. He coined the terms Theory X and Theory Y to describe these categories of worker.

Theory X suggests that workers are lazy and reluctant to work. Theory Y on the other hand states that workers prefer autonomy and responsibility and gain a sense of achievement from their work.

THEORY X	THEORY Y
Workers are lazy	Workers are keen
Workers need pushed	Workers work on their own
Workers avoid responsibility	Workers seek responsibility
Workers have no initiative	Workers seek to show initiative
Workers respond to threats	Workers respond to rewards
Workers are motivated by money	Workers have a range of different needs

MOTIVATION

This work was based on Maslow's theory and suggested that Theory X workers are those who would appear at the lower levels of the hierarchy, whereas Theory Y workers would appear at the top levels.

From a motivational perspective, if workers are thought to fall under the Theory X category, then the only way to get them to perform is to use coercion and threats. This method is often referred to as the stick approach. The major problem with adopting this method of management is that management needs to be very careful not to break employment laws or company-wide agreements.

Theory Y would take the opposite approach and allow workers to get on with the job, creating a culture where they will get involved in the work and make valid contributions.

Various studies have revealed that managers tend to see themselves as Theory Y workers and their subordinates as Theory X workers. However, in practice their behaviour is closer to Theory X. Furthermore, there appears to be a link between Theory X and Theory Y and an employee's position on the organisational chart. Workers lower down tend to be more motivated by things such as money than workers who are higher up the chain.

TASK

Evaluate a firm's decision to adopt McGregor's approach to employee motivation.

HERZBERG'S TWO FACTOR THEORY

In 1966 Frederick Herzberg analysed the job attitudes of 200 accountants and engineers who were asked to describe when they had felt positive or negative at work and the reasons why.

From this research, Herzberg divided these factors into two categories, which he labelled Motivators and Hygiene Factors.

Motivator factors

Motivator factors are those that give workers job satisfaction. If they are effective, then they can motivate an individual to improve their performance and effort.

Motivators include:

- Status
- Opportunity for advancement
- Gaining recognition
- Responsibility
- Challenging/stimulating work
- Sense of personal achievement and personal growth in a job

Hygiene factors

Hygiene factors, if they are absent, can cause dissatisfaction with work. If these factors are improved, dissatisfaction in the workplace should be reduced. However, it is important to note that hygiene factors alone are not likely to motivate an individual.

Hygiene factors include:

- Company policy and administration

- Wages, salaries and other financial remuneration

- Quality of supervision

- Quality of interpersonal relations

- Working conditions

- Feelings of job security

There is some similarity between Herzberg's and Maslow's work. They both suggest that an employee is motivated when their needs are satisfied. However, Herzberg argues that only the higher levels of the Maslow Hierarchy (eg self-actualisation, esteem needs) act as a motivator. The remaining needs can only cause dissatisfaction if not addressed.

Herzberg's Two Factor Theory		
Hygiene Factors		**Motivators**
Salary, Job Security, Working Conditions, Level and Quality of Supervision, Company Policy and Administration, Interpersonal Relations		Nature of Work, Sense of Achievement, Recognition, Responsibility, Personal Growth and Advancement

Herzberg argued that both factors are equally important, but that good hygiene will only lead to average performance and prevent dissatisfaction. To motivate employees, management must assess the content of the actual work that they do and try to introduce a motivator, eg giving employees a greater level of responsibility.

Herzberg and money

It is often wrongly claimed that Herzberg did not value money since he did not classify it as a motivator. This is misleading, as Herzberg argues that if good hygiene factors, including money, are missing, this will lead to dissatisfaction and thus make it difficult to motivate the worker.

These original studies have been repeated with different types of workers, and results have proved consistent with the original research. Despite this, Herzberg's theory has been criticised. It has been argued that one factor may be a satisfier for one person, but cause job dissatisfaction for another. For example, increased responsibility may be welcomed by some, whilst opposed by others. Meanwhile, the existence of hygiene factors can remove satisfaction at first, but can then be taken for granted, resulting in the need for improvements in the future. For instance, adequate pay can remove dissatisfaction at first, but once this has been awarded, improved pay will be expected in following years. It has also been argued that the redesigning of jobs can be costly to implement.

Despite these criticisms, Herzberg has highlighted the importance of job design in trying to motivate the workforce. (See page 36)

TASK

Evaluate a firm's decision to adopt Herzberg's approach to employee motivation.

MONETARY METHODS OF MOTIVATION

From the motivation theories that we have outlined, it is obvious that there is no consensus as to what exactly motivates workers. The scientific approach advocated by Taylor, Maslow's physiological needs, and McGregor's Theory X, would argue that workers respond to financial rewards. Even Herzberg believes that without an adequate pay structure, workers will be demotivated. It is therefore important to recognise the impact of financial rewards upon employees. This poses the question: how should workers be financially rewarded for their efforts?

Time rates

This system rewards employees for the amount of time that they spend on work. It is calculated by multiplying the number of hours that an employee works by the hourly rate of pay. The major advantage of this system is that workers do not need to rush what they are doing, and so the quality of the product is not impaired. However, the downside of this is that workers have no incentive to work hard and time-wasting can actually occur. This

could have an even more detrimental effect if the time-wasting results in the employee being given overtime to complete a task. Sometimes this overtime may be paid at a higher rate than employees usually receive. Another advantage of time rates is that it is useful when employees are working in groups, or for people working in the service sector where there is no actual product to produce. Time rates are used in situations where an employee has no control over the speed of the work carried out, and in cases where the product is not a standardised one.

Piece rates

This system rewards an employee according to the quantity of items that an individual (or group of workers) produces. This system ensures that employees are rewarded for what they actually do. Piece rate is sometimes referred to as 'payments by results' because employees have the opportunity to increase their pay if they produce more. However, this can lead to employees rushing work or taking shortcuts, which can result in sub standard products being produced. For products that are standardised, this is an ideal way of rewarding employees, although the output must be measurable. Also, if quality control is introduced to ensure that shortcuts are not being taken, the issue of quality can be resolved. However, if a machine breaks down or if an employee is part of an assembly line that stops, there is the possibility that the employee could be penalised through no fault of their own. Trade unions do not support this method of pay as they believe it can lead to low pay and low living standards. Some would argue that the rates set are sometimes inappropriate.

TASK

> List the advantages and disadvantages of using Piece Rates and Time Rates as a method of rewarding employees.

Commission

Commission is similar to piece rates in that it rewards employees for the quantity or value of work that they sell. This method rewards employees by giving them a percentage of the value of the work that is sold. It can be argued that it is unfair to employees as it does not take into account the amount of effort that they make, but that it is linked to what is actually sold. Research has shown that this method of remuneration is in decline – the proportion of people's earnings made up of commission has fallen. However, this method is still important in industrial sectors such as insurance where it provides an incentive for sales people to try to sell more of a product or service.

Fees

Fees are one-off payments made to employees for one-off tasks. The amount paid will depend on a number of factors, such as the time taken to do the task, the complexity of the task, and the skills required to complete the task.

Fringe benefits

These are benefits that may be given to employees, such as a company pension scheme, a company car, or free private medical insurance. Some of these benefits may be welcome to employees from a taxation point of view, although in recent years the benefits are not as great as they once were.

Profit sharing

This involves employees receiving a share of the company's profits at the end of the financial year. These schemes have many advantages in that they provide an incentive for employees to work harder, and can also reduce staff turnover. However, if the organisation does not make high levels of profit, employees will receive little or nothing. This can demotivate staff. Profit sharing schemes tend to reward all employees equally, irrespective of how much effort individuals contributed to the organisation's performance.

Performance-related pay

These schemes link an employee's annual salary to their performance. They have grown in popularity in recent years as organisations try to increase flexibility in the workplace. Performance can be measured in a number of ways, such as comparing an individual's actual performance with their agreed targets. There are different ways of making the payment which can range from the payment of a bonus at the end of the year to the award of an increment on the employee's pay scale. Although performance-related pay can motivate workers to perform better, they will not work if the reward is not perceived as valuable to the employee. Problems can also arise in situations where it may be difficult to measure performance accurately.

MOTIVATION

Drawbacks of incentive schemes and monetary methods of motivation

Incentive schemes that attempt to encourage more efficient and more productive work can have many drawbacks. As already mentioned, workers may not be able to achieve targets through no fault of their own. For instance, if an employee is working on an assembly line and the line goes down, the worker may fail to meet the targets that were agreed. There could also be changes in the external environment that may result in changes in demand for the product or service. In such cases, the employee has no control over the achievement of targets. Quality can also suffer if employees become reliant on an incentive scheme. If there is pressure to achieve targets, these may be pursued by taking shortcuts or cutting corners. Unhealthy staff relationships can also develop if employees become jealous of others and resent the payments being made to them.

TASK

Evaluate the effectiveness of different financial incentives as a way of motivating workers.

NON-MONETARY METHODS OF MOTIVATION AND JOB DESIGN

The motivation theories studied earlier highlighted the fact that not all employees are necessarily motivated by money. As a result of this, it is important for an organisation to clearly identify what other factors motivate the workforce and look for ways of trying to meet these needs. These developments have resulted in organisations giving consideration to job design as a means of increasing job satisfaction for employees.

If job design or in fact job redesign is to be successful, some basic principles must be considered:

- The job must be meaningful and employees need to feel a sense of achievement.
- Job design should provide a degree of autonomy for workers. This should include the ability of workers to take responsibility for quality and a choice of how they carry out tasks.
- Job design should provide employees with the opportunity to work as a member of a team and allow interaction between fellow employees.
- The job should provide variety for the employee, including the ability to carry out a range of tasks.

It is interesting to note how different these principles are to Taylor's scientific management approach.

When designing or redesigning a job, a variety of approaches may be adopted. Although there are different methods of doing this, the main ones adopted by organisations are job enlargement, job rotation, and job enrichment.

Job enlargement

Job enlargement involves giving employees more to do and creating greater scope and variety within the job. Employees are less likely to get bored if they a range of tasks rather than repeating the same thing over and over. They may also derive more satisfaction from the job if they are allowed to complete an entire task rather than one part of it.

The major criticism of job enlargement is that employees may see it as an attempt to increase their work load by requiring them to carry out more tasks at the same level.

Likewise, if the tasks are of a similar nature, job design may have no impact whatsoever on reducing boredom. It may also be argued that job enlargement ignores the benefits that may be achieved through job specialisation, and efficiency may in fact decline.

Job rotation

Job rotation involves an employee changing tasks or jobs in an attempt to reduce boredom and increase motivation. If employees are moving between tasks, it also means that they can become multi-skilled, which is an advantage to the organisation. However, the downside of this is that, productivity may be lost if employees need to be trained to carry out new tasks. It can also be argued that employees will continue to get bored if they are simply rotated from one boring job to another.

Job enrichment

Job enrichment gives employees greater responsibility by allowing them to have more autonomy and more participation in the decision-making process. Job enrichment gives employees a challenge and makes them feel that they are part of the organisation. Job enrichment also allows employees to make decisions about methods and the sequence of work, and increases their individual responsibility. Despite these advantages, job enrichment has been criticised as a way of cutting the workforce because it requires workers to carry out extra tasks. Ultimately, not all workers want to have more responsibility and might in fact find this demotivating.

Team working

Team working involves establishing teams to meet production goals. The members of these teams decide between themselves how the work should be distributed and how problem-solving should take place.

Quality circles

Quality circles are groups of employees who meet on a regular basis to discuss production techniques and make suggestions as to how production problems might be solved. The major advantage of this approach is that employees are directly involved in the work that they are carrying out. Although quality circles have their roots in Japan, they are now widely used by organisations in the UK. The major disadvantage of quality circles is that they only work if they have the full support of both managers and employees.

Empowerment

Empowerment is like delegation. It is when power or authority is given to employees so they can make their own decisions regarding their working life. For example, workers have control over how to use their time and decide the priority of tasks that need to be done. They are encouraged to confront problems and come up with some solutions.

For empowerment to be successful, workers must have adequate training and/or good skill levels in order to be trusted to make the correct decisions. If they do not, then expensive mistakes can be made that could affect the whole business. It is the manager's job to judge whether a subordinate can cope with more authority and decision-making power. It should be noted however, that even if managers pass down authority to their subordinates, they are still responsible for the work that is done by them.

TASK

Evaluate the effectiveness of different non-monetary methods of motivating workers.

CASE STUDY

MOTIVATING YOUR STAFF

SAP is the largest producer of business software in the world.

Motivating its staff is a big job as it has some 29,000 of them in 50 different countries, and yet it claims to be among the best at doing this.

Indeed SAP has won awards for its innovative ways of keeping its staff happy. It starts with the most obvious incentive of all – money. After all, ask most people why they work and they'll answer in order to get paid and make a living and at SAP the staff are very well rewarded indeed.

"Our average basic salary here is around £45,000," says Adrian Farley, human resources director at SAP.

"It's a very good package and our staff enjoy exceptional benefits, as well as a bonus scheme, but we're competing for the very best people out there and often they will dictate their own terms."

Flexibility

Unlike a manufacturer which may see its machinery or equipment as its most valuable asset, SAP's success as a business depends fully on the brainpower of its employees and their ability to serve its clients – hence its efforts to keep them happy.

SAP has tried to create a flexible working environment and an incentive-based pay structure is designed to improve overall operational performance and productivity. To motivate and encourage, every employee's package includes fixed, flexible and incentive-based portions. The flexible portion of each salary can be used to buy and sell annual leave, for dental or medical services, for pensions, life assurance and concierge services.

Pleasant offices

Furthermore, workers are provided with free lunch in the top-class restaurant, and the building is designed to encourage team-work and creativity. Staff and their families are given private dental and health care, and access to other services like dry-cleaning.

"The coffee lounges and workspaces are nice and bright throughout the building and this is good for teamwork," says Rachel Cortes, a customer relations manager.

"It cheers you up, and we've also got flexible benefits so I can buy holiday time or choose to contribute more to my pension, and a lot of the benefits are extended to family too."

But what if you're not a giant software conglomerate, and still want your staff to enjoy working for you?

Taking pride

Take Savoir Beds in west London for instance. It's a much smaller, more traditional manufacturing business, but still has its own unique ways of motivating its workers.

Savoir has been making beds since 1905; each one costs £6,000 and it produces only six a week, so speed isn't the priority, quality is. "Rather than have a production line with workers just operating on one part of the bed we actually encourage them to do the whole thing", says Alastair Hughes, managing director of Savoir Beds.

CASE STUDY...

Workers here don't get bonuses for making more beds quicker, and the firm could not afford to match the salaries that SAP pays for example. "Bonuses don't work here; instead we want the staff to take pride in what they do by working on the product from start to finish," says Alastair.

Work of art

"Rather than have a production line with workers just operating on one part of the bed we actually encourage them to do the whole thing, and then when it's finished we ask them to sign the bed. Customers come in and meet the staff."

Customers write thank you letters to the person who made their bed, and everyone in the business has a sense of pride in what they do.

The personal approach

At Savoir Beds there is recognition that staff are human beings whose needs differ – so the approach needs to be flexible. SAP has a flexible remuneration package, a mix of fixed, flexible and incentive-based parts.

The flexible part allows people to choose from these benefits:

- choice to take pay instead of holiday and visa versa
- dental care
- medical care
- pensions
- life assurance

It allows people to start early, finish late, work part-time for a period, have a sabbatical or take periods of unpaid leave. Staff are encouraged to contribute their ideas. They even come back from holidays with bed catalogues!

The organisation is 'flat' so there are few layers of management. Benefits packages are common to all. The best benefits are not reserved for the top level staff. The difference comes from salaries and bonuses – which are earned through incentive schemes.

The business has a strong bonus/reward culture so people expect those who do well to be paid well. There are no 'fat cat' secrets. Everyone is on the same terms. They each have a contract – and no more.

If senior management fail they won't get a big pay-off when they are pushed out! The staff have asked to see how the system works and SAP is working on making everything as transparent as possible. The needs of the multicultural workforce are also well catered for. All religious requirements are respected.

SAP and Savoir are two very different companies, but what they both make is an effort to motivate their workforce. The success of both businesses genuinely depends on it.

Source: BBC NEWS: http://news.bbc.co.uk/go/pr/fr/-/1/hi/programmes/working_lunch/2988186.stm
Published: 13/6/2003

CASE STUDY...

Questions

1. Why is it important to motivate staff?
2. Why can it be easier for a big company to motivate staff than a small one?
3. With reference to a business that you know, explain how it motivates its staff.
4. How does the choice of benefits give opportunities to different sorts of people, young and old, married and single, parents and non-parents?
5. How does the mix of incentives – to earn greater financial reward and the non-financial rewards – stimulate staff to achieve?
6. What benefits are there for staff and the business when one person makes a product from start to finish?
7. In what type of business does this system work well?
8. In what type of business is it not possible?
9. Why do staff find a thank you letter rewarding?
10. What evidence is there that staff have 'ownership' of the product and their role in the business?
11. Work out how both businesses fit into Maslow's Hierarchy of Needs.

CASE STUDY

DOMINO'S

Motivation: how to keep your staff on side

Chris Moore, chief executive of pizza franchise Domino's in the UK and Ireland, believes the key to success is knowing what motivates your staff. And he is happy to dress up to get them on his side ... his starring roles include the Queen, film icon Marilyn Monroe, blue-coiffed cartoon character Marge Simpson and Star Trek's stern-faced but sexy Lieutenant Uhura. Not women with much in common, it would seem. But they've all appeared at Domino's Pizza staff parties, albeit in the guise of chief executive Chris Moore.

Since the 1960s, staff have got together to belt out the company chant – "Who are we? Domino's Pizza. What are we? Number one. What's our goal? Sell more pizza, have more fun."

Moore, who has been with Domino's for 18 years, is a firm believer in fun. He gets up in the morning and looks forward to coming to work and believes that his staff do, too. And he's certainly selling more pizza – £18.7m-worth, pre-tax, for the year ending 31 December 2007 – a third up on the previous year.

CASE STUDY...

A people business

Domino's is based on a simple proposition – delivering a great pizza in 30 minutes – which Moore says is extraordinarily difficult to implement. The company relies on its franchisees, having sold off its remaining Domino's-owned stores. There are 514 franchised stores in the UK and Ireland and the plan is to increase that to 1,000 by 2017.

There are 300 members of staff, based at its Milton Keynes headquarters and at smaller facilities in Penrith, which serves areas from the Midlands to Inverness, and at Naas, in County Kildare, which serves stores in Ireland. And franchisees and their employees bring the number of team members to 12,000. Hitting the 1,000 stores target will require an increase in support staff (based at the three centres) by up to 500 and a rise in team members to 25,000.

Asked for evidence of his commitment to the people in his business, Moore talks at length and with pride of the rigorous selection process for franchisees.

Apart from showing they have money to invest (£240,000 for the first store, dropping to £190,000 for subsequent outlets), potential franchisees have to go through an initial interview with the franchise sales team, then spend a minimum of a week working in a Domino's Pizza store, before a final interview with a panel that, nine times out of 10, will include the chief executive. Successful franchisees sign up for a decade, and as Moore says: "We need to live with these people for 10 years, so why take the chance?"

He admits, however, that this attention to detail hasn't always been present. "We have gone through different stages in the past where our intention was to get as many franchisees as possible, to open up stores in different places. Now we're at a different stage in our growth where we need to ensure that, from now on, every store that we bring into the Domino's fold is a quality addition to the group."

Another consideration is managing the company's growth. By 2017, Moore intends his 1,000 stores to be operated by a maximum of 200 franchisees. He wants neither the one-store only people nor the portfolio investors. He's looking for dedicated team members who buy into the Domino's culture, who are looking for the American dream, but in the UK or Ireland.

Unlike many chief executives, Moore remains upbeat about recruitment challenges, saying that although he would have agreed that they existed in 2004, he sees less and less of a problem today. He feels there will always be migrant workers keen to work in catering, but admits: "It will be interesting to see what the government does with its immigration policy."

Having more fun

Moore concedes that keeping franchisees engaged is relatively easy, given their own financial and emotional commitment to Domino's – not to mention their signature on the contract.

MOTIVATION

CASE STUDY...

Head office staff are offered what Moore considers "a generous package" – including complimentary massages twice a month. As part of the 'having more fun' sentiment, Domino's throws two annual staff parties – Armageddon Junior and Armageddon Senior, which involves up to 400 revellers and focuses on recognition and reward.

And each year Domino's gives Rolex watches to those staff who have made the most outstanding contribution to the business.

Previous watch winners have included the pizza chef responsible for coming up with new menu combinations and an IT worker responsible for a development that brought substantial cost savings.

Moore believes his staff enjoy coming to work because of the autonomy they're given, while acknowledging that not everyone – or every role – is suited to it. He is convinced that the high level of autonomy stems mainly from the length of time people stay with Domino's – the average tenure in the three top management tiers is nine years.

Key role for HR

Domino's has a small HR team, just seven people, headed by director Jane Roberts. The team deals with the office-based staff, becoming involved with the franchisees only in the case of what Moore refers to as "people issues". He believes HR should be represented on company boards and demonstrates HR's importance to Domino's through the role the team will have to play in the planned expansion.

At the beginning of 2007 the management team realised that, although it had done well to establish a system of benefits for head office staff, it wouldn't be possible to replicate this for franchisees. The team set about establishing an employee brand and recruited someone to promote it to the store-based staff.

Feeling the heat

Last year, Domino's was lambasted for its treatment of foreign franchisees and their staff, and Moore and his team have been quick to implement measures that will help them avoid a repeat performance. Key among these is the company's work with HR and health and safety consultancy, MJL, which has been brought in to manage procedures, including the provision of a 24-hour franchisee advice line and indemnity against any advice provided.

Domino's team members will also be able to access an e-learning package and an online reporting and information system that will help ensure that franchisees are compliant with legislation.

Much of the information is available in franchisees' native languages – Moore is insistent that there can be no room for misinterpretation. He is philosophical about an incident

CASE STUDY...

last year, where it was claimed Hungarian staff were being exploited, pointing out that it was bound to happen to someone in the catering sector. He claims the new system leaves Domino's in a great position, with a system that is "way more advanced than anything else".

Moore sees political correctness in the workplace as "an unfortunate reality of what today's business world has become".

One of his key frustrations surrounding HR professionals is that they are spending so much time dealing with petty issues that they can't see the wood for the trees.

"Great HR people," he says, "have the ability to stand back and take much more of a helicopter view of the situation." And the best piece of advice he's ever been given by an HR director? That would be "count to 10" – or possibly "sleep on it – and rewrite it in the morning".

Source: Tara Craig, www.PersonnelToday.com 19 June 2008

Questions

a) Analyse how Domino's approach fits in with any of the motivation theories that you have studied.

b) Evaluate Domino's approach to staff motivation.

CASE STUDY

Sainsbury's staff slam 'Shining Stars' reward scheme

Sainsbury's staff have reportedly criticised a plan to reward them with 'gold stars'.

The move is one of a number of HR initiatives the supermarket chain is introducing in a bid to improve low staff morale.

But one employee told the Daily Mirror: "It's a joke... the idea they are going to award us gold stars if we're good. What do they think we are – primary school kids?

"How about talking about pay and giving us back the Christmas bonus? That might motivate people better than some Mickey Mouse scheme."

Staff awarded 'Shining Stars' points will be able to redeem them for items in a gift catalogue. Under another scheme, Tell Justin, workers will be urged to devise efficiency or savings ideas.

The initiatives form part of a business shake-up that is designed to boost sales by £2.5bn over the next three years.

Source: Dan Thomas, www.PersonnelToday.com 21 October 2004

Question

Analyse why workers at Sainsbury's may not find this approach motivational.

CASE STUDY

Do benefits packages score with staff?

A recent survey reveals that organisations have not got to grips with how best to motivate and retain staff using benefits packages despite clear evidence that they can work wonders with morale.

A recent survey reveals that organisations have not got to grips with how best to motivate and retain staff using benefits packages despite clear evidence that they can work wonders with morale.

Private health insurance, share options, company car, pension scheme, gym membership – there is little doubt that what employers like to call a 'generous package' looks great in a job advertisement.

But does this multitude of benefits really help motivate and retain staff? Do employees actually make use of their benefits? Do they want them at all?

A survey of almost 750 UK firms across all sectors suggests the answers to these questions are far from clear. More than a quarter of companies surveyed offering standard benefits packages felt the major issue they faced was that it wasn't sufficiently valued by staff.

Difficulty in communicating a benefits package was a key issue for more than a fifth of firms, while 16 % thought their package was too costly, and 15 % believed it required too much administration.

Michael Whitfield, managing director of Thomson Online Benefits, which commissioned the survey, said the findings show that firms can make their benefits strategies more effective. Better communication should result in better take-up and appreciation of benefits, he said. But, of course, no amount of good communication will persuade staff to appreciate benefits they do not want.

"Gym membership is the classic," said Whitfield. "There are some people who are never going to go to the gym, regardless of how well you sell it. Similarly, childless people do not want discounted crèche facilities, but may appreciate a higher pension scheme contribution.

"You have to look at your workforce and take a view on whether you have the right benefits strategy in place," he added. The survey suggests there are signs that this is beginning to happen. Flexible benefit schemes – where staff are given a degree of choice about what type and level of benefits they receive – are becoming more popular.

However, what change is occurring is slow paced. Only 5 % of organisations have a flexible benefits scheme in place, although a further 10 % are actively considering introducing such a scheme.

Mobile phone company O2 is one organisation that decided against a flexible scheme. Andrew Harley, group HR director, said: "We looked at introducing a flexible benefits scheme after our staff asked us to consider it, but we quickly found the cost of administering such a scheme was too much.

CASE STUDY

"We decided it was better to spend the time getting our pension scheme into shape and concentrating on our core benefits, rather than letting our employees choose and manage their own benefits." Harley said O2 offered its staff the core benefits of a pension scheme, subsidised restaurant and discounted gym membership. The company also provides discounts on mobile phones and O2-sponsored clothing, such as Arsenal football tops and England rugby jerseys. He said that staff were more than happy with this arrangement: "We have conducted focus groups and formal conversations with staff – most want the cash and core benefits rather than other options."

But Harley agreed that communication was vital in the management of any scheme. "We are in the process of launching a website that will provide all staff with their benefit statements online," he said.

"We are also communicating with our employees by issuing new pension benefits statements that give employees a clear understanding of the value of their scheme and the choices open to them."

But Mark Childs, vice-president of reward at the Chartered Institute of Personnel and Development (CIPD), said the extension of technology – especially the internet – has made the cost of administering a flexible benefits scheme more affordable for employers. The momentum behind flexible benefits has increased, said Childs, but companies still need to be thorough when considering such a scheme. "Be clear about the reasons for introducing a scheme," he said. "Invest heavily in the design and planning – don't rush it. And don't underestimate the importance of communication on an ongoing basis."

Source: www.PersonnelToday.com 23 March 2004

Questions

a) Explain why communication is important when seeking to motivate staff.

b) Analyse O2's decision to offer a flexible benefits scheme to its employees.

CASE STUDY

Online benefits double take-up at software firm

A software firm has doubled the number of staff taking up company pensions after overhauling its benefits package and putting it online.

Firstwave, a software and management systems company, overhauled its benefits package in a bid to increase take-up among staff.

Amanda Brooker, finance and administration manager, said the review of the company's benefits arrangements had paid dividends.

"Take-up of the pension scheme has gone from 50 % to 100 % of employees. Staff now have access to view and manage their benefits online, and can receive advice and help in person or over the telephone," she explained.

The review was launched to improve participation among the company's predominantly young workforce and reduce the time spent on administering benefits.

Following a joint review with Thomson Online Benefits, Firstwave decided to change the pensions scheme to one with lower running costs, and also put the whole package online. Employees now receive an information pack and meet with an adviser to get help choosing and accessing their benefits. They also have access to a series of interactive web tools to help them choose the most appropriate strategy.

"Our benefit package was not doing what it was supposed to," Brooker said. "Primarily, we wanted to increase the appreciation and take-up of benefits, particularly the pension scheme.

"We felt it was important to improve communication so that employees understood their benefits and recognised the value of the company's investment in them," Brooker said. "Firstwave also viewed the benefits shake-up as an opportunity for the company to demonstrate our commitment to staff."

Source: Mike Berry, www.PersonnelToday.com 23 May 2008

Questions

a) Analyse the impact of technology on communications within Firstwave.

b) Analyse the use of a company pension scheme as a way of motivating staff.

CCEA SPECIMEN QUESTION - SUMMER 07 A2 1

1 Read the information below and answer the questions that follow.

Motivation

Flightneeds plc is a manufacturer of aircraft seating. Over the last five years they have had three redundancy programmes due to the general downturn in the aircraft industry. Existing workers are worried about their jobs and morale is very low. This has resulted in poor delivery and inferior quality of products. More than 50% of deliveries are over 14 days late and poor quality output is costing the company £500,000 per year.

Samuel Jackson has recently been appointed as the new managing director of the company. His first announcement when he arrived was a reassurance to staff that there would be no further redundancies. He claimed that he could improve company performance by motivating staff using non-monetary methods. He was aware that the previous managing director had been a strict believer in Gregor's Theory X. He suspected that this had demotivated the workforce.

Samuel has advised his management team that jobs need to be redesigned. He has suggested that they should consider the principles of job rotation, job enlargement and job enrichment as part of this process. However, some managers are very uncertain about this new approach to managing the workforce.

(a) Explain two reasons why a motivated workforce is necessary for a company such as Flightneeds plc. [4]

(b) Discuss the implications for the employees of Flightneeds plc of the previous managing director adopting a Theory X approach. [8]

Chapter 7: PRINCIPLES OF MANAGEMENT AND LEADERSHIP

MANAGEMENT VERSUS LEADERSHIP

TASK

Use Wikipedia to find the entry for 'leadership'. Scroll down to 'Leadership's relation with management' and discuss the following:

- The qualities needed to be an effective leader
- The differences or similarities, if any, between a leader and a manager

Leadership means different things to different people. To some, George W Bush represents strong and decisive leadership in difficult times; to others, he is a megalomaniac making decisions based on appeasing the interests of businesses in the US.

It should be clear that the main difference between a manager and a leader is the ability of a leader to influence others. This ability can arise as a result of the person's expertise or may be something that the person has been born with. Ideally managers should have leadership qualities, but unfortunately this does not always happen. If a manager is to be effective, he or she should try to adopt leadership qualities so that subordinates become followers, not just another resource to be managed.

MANAGEMENT STYLES

We have discussed in the previous chapter the importance of motivating employees using both financial and non-financial means. Another important factor that must be considered is the management style that is adopted, and the fact that different styles have both advantages and disadvantages.

Authoritarian management

The authoritarian manager makes all of the decisions for employees. Once objectives have been set by the manager, employees are expected to carry out the tasks exactly as the manager has stated. Under this approach, employees often become dependent on the manager as it is he or she who has made all of the decisions. Employees need high levels of supervision and are often demotivated when working in these conditions. Due to the nature of the approach and the environment it creates, employees often have a poor working relationship with the manager.

Despite these drawbacks, authoritarian management is essential in certain situations, such as in the army where orders need to be obeyed without questions being asked. This style of management may also be appropriate in situations where employees are not self-motivated and prefer structure in their job-related activities.

Paternalistic management

The paternalistic manager dictates to employees what to do, although these actions are for the benefit of the employees rather than the organisation. The idea behind this type of management is that although an authoritarian approach is being used, the negatives, such as lack of motivation amongst employees, can be reduced. If such an approach is used, it can have many advantages such as loyalty to management. However, there can be over reliance on the manager and if wrong decisions are made, employees can become dissatisfied.

David Brent, from the BBC Sitcom the Office, is the type of boss who wants to be everyone's friend and mentor. He imagines that everyone finds him very funny and loves being around him, yet still respects him and looks up to him as a boss and even a father figure. In reality his staff are often embarrassed by his behaviour.

You might want to watch an episode from The Office in order to examine this approach to management.

Democratic management

The democratic manager allows employees to take part in the decision-making process and they are consulted and involved in decision-making. This style of management allows employees to be clear about the aims and objectives of the organisation and because staff are involved in how these are achieved, they will be motivated to work on behalf of the organisation. This style of management is particularly suited to organisations that have a flat structure. In organisations which have tall structures, the different layers can make communication difficult, and this can hamper the process. The major disadvantage of this style of management is that the consultation process can be time-consuming and there is the danger that managerial control may be lost. It is important to note that this style of management requires a manager who has strong communication skills.

Laissez-faire

Laissez-faire comes from the French language and means 'leave well alone'. This style allows employees to carry out their work without any interference from management, which results in an environment where there are few restrictions. In some circumstances this can result in employees having little incentive to work. However, this approach is useful in industries where creativity and innovation are important, such as in software development.

FACTORS AFFECTING MANAGEMENT STYLES

The type of management style adopted will depend on various factors:

- *The task.* If a decision needs to be taken quickly, there may not be any time for consultation. Therefore, an authoritarian style might be needed.
- *The culture of the organisation.* A culture can develop over the lifespan of an organisation and this may influence the type of style adopted. Therefore, it may be difficult to break with traditions or, the actual administrative set-up in an organisation may dictate the style used.
- *The type of labour force.* If the workforce is highly skilled or highly motivated, they may welcome consultation. However, an unskilled workforce may only respond to an authoritarian style.
- *The group size.* If the group of workers is very large, it may be difficult to allow a democratic style to emerge.
- *The manager's personality.* Different managers may have different personalities and this will play a major part in the management style adopted. Some managers may feel uncomfortable with certain management styles.

CASE STUDY

MANAGEMENT STYLES: TOO CRUEL TO BE KIND

The Apprentice is compulsive viewing, but could Sir Alan Sugar's 'firm' management style work for other employers?

Forget Big Brother, macho managers are the latest TV sensation. From effing Gordon Ramsay on Hell's Kitchen to entrepreneur Sir Alan Sugar on The Apprentice announcing, "I am the most belligerent person you could ever meet", it's compulsive television.

But is it good HR practice? Probably not. While tough management styles are sometimes appropriate – in highly-pressurised work environments such as the NHS, the Armed Forces,

PRINCIPLES OF MANAGEMENT AND LEADERSHIP

CASE STUDY...

the entertainment industry and in the City, for instance – legal and occupational psychology experts agree that there's a fine line between assertive management, which gets results, and bullying, which destroys staff morale.

Context is important, says David Whincup, head of the London employment department of law firm Hammonds.

Under pressure

"In a City dealing room, people rightly or wrongly tend to put up with a lot of abuse – it's a 'live fast, die young' culture. It's also true that the more senior you are, the more flak you are expected to be able to take."
Situation can be an even more decisive factor. Melody Blackburn, principal consultant with organisational psychology firm OPP, says: "If a high level of control is needed – in a start-up or business turn-around, for example – an assertive management style is effective.
In a crisis, decisions need to be made quickly."
But employers need to be aware of the potential legal consequences of this 'cruel to be kind' approach to management, even if they are not clear-cut.

Whincup says: "You can't be taken to court for bullying itself. The employee has to prove that the bullying has some legal consequences – for example, that you usually bully women or you are making people ill by your treatment of them."

Either way, this is not an issue that HR can casually ignore. Sarah Veale, head of equality and employment rights at the TUC, believes The Apprentice is a negative influence. "It's nauseating," she says. "The Sir Alan Sugar line is to test people to do their jobs well under pressure. But people aren't more effective under this kind of pressure – they don't do well, they get sick."

TUC statistics back this up: a 2005 survey calculated that bullying accounted for the loss of 18 million working days per year, and another TUC survey of more than 5,000 employees found that managers were responsible for 75% of bullying incidents.

Sue Scates, vice-president of support services for IT company Oracle in the UK, Ireland and South Africa, points out that leaders need more than one way of motivating staff. "You need to invest in employee learning and development, and it's critical that their leader instils a good sense of teamwork, rather than playing staff off against each other."

Soft skills

Faced with a wannabe Sir Alan Sugar among the management ranks, what role should HR take? Experts agree that a softly-softly approach is advisable.

Sally Bibb, author of The Stone Age Company: Why the companies we work for are dying and how they can be saved, has years of senior HR experience in the telecoms industry, and came across a whole range of aggressive bosses during that time.

PRINCIPLES OF MANAGEMENT AND LEADERSHIP

CASE STUDY...

"Out of almost 20 managers, only two were personally effective," she says now. "My most memorable Stone Age boss was known to the entire company as a bully – even the CEO knew about it. But it was just accepted. He shouted and raged at people, often reducing staff to tears, and he rejoiced in that."

After a while, Bibb decided that it would help the bullying boss if he was made aware of the effect he was having. So she had a quiet word with him. "I honestly thought 'no-one is telling this guy what people think, and no-one is doing him any favours by not telling him'. And, of course, he exploded. The trouble is that people don't know themselves, and they don't want to."

Cary Cooper, Professor of Organisational Psychology at Lancaster University Management School, believes HR can only have a limited impact if bullying is part of the organisational culture. Senior managers have a major part to play in forming this culture – and Sugar illustrates this. "His approach makes people so sycophantic," says Cooper. "Everyone is trying to please him. They will do anything to put people down. The attitude is 'I am going to get ahead'. There is nothing about team-building or trust."

But how effective can HR be in countering this? Whincup observes that, because HR is often viewed as the mouthpiece of the management, there's little it can do if the manager in question won't learn or apologise when appropriate.

"There isn't much HR can do except try some training both to pre-empt the behaviour in question and to form a defence if it happens anyway," Whincup advises.

Don't make it dull
But that doesn't mean leaders can't be dynamic and push staff to stretch themselves. Emmanuel Gobillot, a director at the Hay Group HR consultancy and author of The Connected Leader, warns against being too prescriptive about management, and making it seem dull. "People look at someone like [celebrity chef] Gordon Ramsay, and think 'I want a bit of what he's got'. I think we have made management seem far too boring, and imposed too much rigidity on people.

"HR needs to build awareness of what is acceptable, promote examples of good practice and look at how people feel and react to what we do," he says.

HR must also ensure its own house is in order. Issuing endless diktats about how to crush bullying, sexual harassment and other ills is simply counter-productive, Blackburn suggests. "Autocratic management can have the effect of making people passive-aggressive – they say they will do things, but they do nothing," she warns.

After all, HR professionals are not exempt from dishing out bully-boy tactics themselves – they can sometimes be the worst offenders. Last month it was revealed that Suzy Walton, a senior civil servant at the Cabinet Office, was subjected to consistent bullying and sexual discrimination within the personnel department. She alleged she was repeatedly undermined, and screamed at by a senior male colleague.

Source: Sally O'Reilly, www.personneltoday.com 25April 2006

Questions
a) Identify and explain the different management styles outlined in the case study.
b) Analyse the possible impact of the management styles identified in the case study.

CASE STUDY

THE MAIN FUNCTIONS OF MANAGEMENT

Henri Fayol

Henri Fayol was one of Europe's leading thinkers on the principles of management. He was one of the earliest people to write and lecture on management issues, and he is sometimes referred to as the first management thinker. Fayol believed that there were a number of functions of management or roles that managers should perform if they were to be successful in their jobs.

The five functions that he identified are as follows:

1. *Planning.* The role of planning requires managers to set aims and objectives as well as putting into place strategies for achieving them.
2. *Organising.* Organisations are very complex. They are often made up of different departments and have a range of people working on various tasks and projects. A manager needs to be able to organise all of these activities so that the organisation can perform as efficiently as possible.
3. *Commanding.* A manager must have the ability to command employees to do what is required. If a manager cannot perform this task, employees will not know what is expected of them.
4. *Coordination.* Due to the complexity of organisations, management need to be able to coordinate all of the activities so that every department and individual is working together.
5. *Controlling.* Management must be able to control the activities that they are directing, which requires them to monitor and measure what is to be achieved. If they are not achieving what they set out to do, they need to take corrective action.

Peter Drucker

Peter Drucker, another management thinker, in his book, *The Practice of Management,* set out his own ideas as to what an effective manager should be able to do.

- *Setting Objectives.* Managers must decide what the organisation's objectives are and what needs to be done to achieve them.
- *Organising.* The manager needs to divide the activities of the organisation into manageable jobs and group these into an organisation structure, selecting the most appropriate people to carry out the jobs.
- *Motivation and communication.* The manager must get the most out of people by trying to motivate them. This is achieved through constant communication, both from manager to subordinate and from subordinate to manager.
- *Measurement.* Performance must be measurable. This allows the manager to make judgements on whether activities and tasks have been successfully performed and if company objectives are being met.
- *Developing People.* The manager brings out the best in employees, strengthening them for the good of the organisation.

TASK

Compare Fayol's functions of management with those outlined by Drucker, highlighting the differences and similarities between the two approaches. Suggest reasons for your findings.

CASE STUDY...

Leadership failings and mistakes: the top 10

Nobody's perfect, not even management, as training specialists the Ken Blanchard Companies found out when they asked 1,400 executives what they think are the biggest mistakes leaders make or failings that leaders possess. They include some old favourites.

1. Failing to provide appropriate feedback, especially praise and redirection.

2. Failing to involve others in processes.

3. Failing to use a leadership style that is appropriate to the personnel, task or situation.

4. Failing to set clear and understood goals and objectives.

5. Failing to train and develop their staff.

6. Inappropriate use of communication, especially listening, and a tendency to ignore alternative viewpoints.

7. A tendency to give too much or too little supervision, direction or delegation.

8. A general lack of management skills, such as problem-solving, decision-making and consensus-building.

9. A tendency to provide too little or inappropriate support.

10. A lack of accountability, especially in holding staff accountable for agreed goals and behaviour.

Source: www.PersonnelToday.com 26 July 2006

TASK

Is there anything that these executives could learn from Henri Fayol and Peter Drucker?

CASE STUDY

During the last 20 or 30 years, a new breed of workers has emerged in the workplace. These workers, sometimes referred to as Generation Y employees, have a different attitude to work than their parents.

Rather than building up their careers over time, these individuals want to make their mark immediately and are dissatisfied if they feel that they have not been given the opportunity to develop or prove themselves.

Generation Y employees tend to be well educated and are self-assured as a result of the opportunities that they have been given when growing up. They are also very independent and feel that they should be judged by their performance and outcomes rather than by the amount of time that they spend on tasks. Generation Y employees do not fit into the traditional 9–5 model of work and expect to be able to leave the workplace once a task has been completed. However, the upside of this is the willingness of such workers to work on tasks from home if it achieves results. The Generation Y employees also try to multi-task by listening to iPods or chat to friends on social network sites while working, but studies have shown that IQ levels drop by 10% if workers are distracted by more than one task.

Generation X workers (those born in the 1960s and 1970s) have a completely different view on working practices, fitting into the 9–5 routine and following very strict and inflexible working practices.

As a result, today's managers are faced with a dilemma. Many of them come from the Generation X school and are in charge of a mix of employees who are both Generation X and Generation Y.

Chapter 5: INVESTING IN PEOPLE

Most medium and large sized organisations have a human resources department which is responsible for managing the firm's employees. The human resources department carries out a range of activities including human resource planning, induction, training, recruitment, selection, and appraisal. This chapter will examine each of these functions and highlight their importance to the effective operation of an organisation.

HUMAN RESOURCE PLANNING

Succession planning

An important role of the human resources department is ensuring that the organisation has the correct staff to enable it to perform effectively. There is a range of issues that the human resources department needs to address if it is to successfully put in place an effective plan. These might include analysing the current employment needs of the organisation, forecasting the future demand for employees, forecasting the future supply of employees and predicting labour turnover. Once these have been considered, the human resources department can then put in place strategies and courses of action to meet these needs.

Planning methods
Analysing the current employment situation

The human resources department needs to examine the current employee needs of the organisation. This may require an examination of the mission and aims of the organisation. If, for example, the organisation's main aim is to provide a high quality product or service, it will need to employ staff with the appropriate skills to meet these objectives. Additionally, the human resources department will need to ensure that there are enough employees currently employed in the organisation to fulfil all the company's tasks. The department will also need to evaluate the age of the current workforce, levels of absenteeism, labour turnover, hours worked per week, and promotion prospects. This information will provide the human resources department with an overall view of the status of employees within the organisation at that time.

Forecasting employee demand

In order to operate effectively, a human resources department needs to predict how many employees the organisation will need in the future. There are different ways of doing this and one method may be to use time series, which is a way of forecasting future needs based on past performance. However, like all forecasting techniques, unexpected changes in the external environment can affect the accuracy of these predictions. Changes in technology, as well as in working practices, can also make it very difficult to predict what skills and qualities employees should have in the future.

Forecasting the future supply of employees

The human resources department will need to examine the current situation in the labour market: the number of employees available with certain skills, the demographics of the local area, and the general qualifications and skills of employees. If the available labour force is not adequate, this may restrict the organisation's ability to meet future aims and objectives. Furthermore, it could mean that the organisation may need to widen its net and look elsewhere for suitable employees. Although demographics can help to forecast potential employee numbers, difficulties can arise if there are changes in the external environment. For example, the increase in the numbers of migrant workers in Northern Ireland in recent times would have been difficult to predict five years ago, and this has impacted on local employment trends.

Other factors that might influence the future supply of employees include the degree of competition for jobs within a local area, new housing developments, and the availability of good transport links for commuting to work.

TASK

How could management motivate generation X and Generation Y workers?

Predicting labour turnover

If current employees leave the firm or if they are promoted, this leaves a vacancy that needs to be filled by the organisation. Therefore, it is in the organisation's interests to predict the labour turnover as this will give an indication of the number of employees that may be needed in the future.

Labour turnover can be calculated by expressing the number of staff leaving as a percentage of those who could have left the organisation.

$$\frac{\textbf{Number of staff leaving per period}}{\textbf{Average number of staff in post during the period}} \times \textbf{100}$$

The result of this calculation can form the basis for possible future labour turnover, which can help the human resources department plan future needs.

PROBLEMS WITH HUMAN RESOURCE PLANNING

Although there are many advantages associated with human resource planning, there are also some limitations that the human resources department needs to consider before fully relying on a plan.

- Human resource planning does not take into consideration the behaviour of employees. It simply seeks to predict the numbers of staff that may be needed in the future. This means that situations may arise where the correct number of employees may have been recruited, but some employees may decide that they simply do not like the job and leave. This may result in periods where the actual human resource requirements of the firm have not been met.

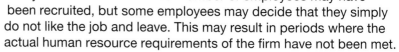

- As previously discussed, changes in the external environment can make it difficult to accurately predict future human resource requirements. Changes in the economic climate can result in periods of economic boom or recession. This can greatly affect the demand for goods and services, which in turn can have an impact on the demand for labour. The recent credit crunch is an excellent example of this. Other changes in the external environment, such as natural disasters or terrorist threats, can also play an important role in affecting the accuracy of human resource plans.

RECRUITMENT

Effective recruitment of staff is essential if an organisation is to make the most of its human resources. The main objective of recruitment from an organisational perspective is to ensure that the best candidates are chosen and retained for a job. If this does not happen, the chosen member of staff may not be capable of carrying out the duties of the post, may become demotivated, and could even leave the organisation. The human resources department should consider three factors when seeking to employ staff.

- What the job actually entails
- The qualities that a person would need to have to do the job correctly
- How staff should be rewarded and motivated

Job analysis

Before the recruitment process can begin, the human resources department needs to be clear about what the job actually entails. To this end, they will conduct a job analysis which will allow them to identify the skills, training and tasks performed in the role. Several factors must be considered by the human resources department when conducting a job analysis:

- Task analysis. This human resources department examines all the individual tasks that an employee needs to perform in order to fulfil the role on offer.
- Activity analysis. This assesses all the physical and intellectual activities that make up an individual task.
- Skills analysis. This looks at the skills that are required to do the overall job. These skills may be of a physical, mental or intellectual nature.
- Role analysis. This examines all of the duties, responsibilities and behaviour expected from a job.
- Performance analysis. This sets out the criteria that assesses how well an employee has performed.

Job analysis allows the human resources department to gain a sound understanding of the requirements of a particular job and it forms the basis of drawing up job descriptions and person specifications.

The Job Description

A job description is a document which outlines the duties and responsibilities associated with a particular job. The following is an example of some of the elements that will be included in a job description.

JOB DESCRIPTION			

POST TITLE	Administration Assistant		
DIVISION/DEPARTMENT	Installation and Facilities Management		
REPORTS TO	Installation and Facilities Manager	GRADE	7

AIM
To provide administrative support within the Specified Group within the Technical Division. The post holder will be required to work flexibly, in a rapidly developing office environment. It may be necessary to assist, or cover for, other administrative staff from time to time.

RESPONSIBILITIES

The key duties of the post are:

- Filing of correspondence
- Setting up and maintaining filing systems as and when required
- Preparing document transmittal forms based on a list of drawings/documents which the Group is required to issue
- Upkeep of the document/drawing register of all the Group contractors who have been sent documents/drawings
- Typing – Word skills for general preparation of letters/forms along with logging into the Group records system
- User notifications for statutory/routine/unplanned for inspections/testing/repairs etc
- Arrange meetings, book and prepare meeting rooms and provide/arrange hospitality
- Helpdesk assistance

Plus other duties consistent with the grade as directed. Because of the changing nature of our business your job description will inevitably change. You will, from time to time, be required to undertake other activities of a similar nature that fall within your capabilities as directed by management.

Essentially, job descriptions outline to potential candidates what is expected of them, and is a source of reference for human resources, especially if there is uncertainty over the remit and responsibilities of the new employee. However, in many cases – such as the job description shown above – a generalised clause is inserted that reminds the employees of the need to be flexible.

The Person Specification

The person specification is drawn up from the job description and it outlines the physical and mental attributes that are required for a particular job. This profile can be used as the basis for selecting the most suitable person for a job:

- Physical appearance
- Intelligence
- Attainments
- Knowledge
- Experience
- Aptitude
- Personality

These requirements may be further sub-divided into essential and desirable requirements. If an applicant does not possess one of the essential requirements, this will automatically make them unsuitable for the job. If there is more than one candidate possessing the essential requirements, the human resources department will examine the desirable requirements to help them to decide on who may be the most appropriate candidate.

PERSON SPECIFICATION Assessment for recruitment requirements and competencies		

JOB TITLE: Administration Assistant

DIVISION/DEPARTMENT: Installation and Facilities Management

LINE MANAGER: Installation and Facilities Manager

		SPECIFY ESSENTIAL(E) DESIRABLE (D)
APTITUDES/ SKILLS/ABILITIES	• Flexible approach to working conditions and change in working environment	E
	• Self-motivated and enthusiastic worker	E
	• Ability to work on own initiative	D
	• Effective team worker	D
QUALIFACTIONS/ KNOWLEDGE AND EXPERIENCE	• GCSE level or equivalent	E
	• Computer literate – Word and Excel in particular	E
	• Good communication skills: verbal/written	E
	• Good problem-solving skills	E
	• Personal work planning and organisational skills	D
	• Experience of working within a site construction team would be advantageous	

TASK

Draw up a Job Description and a Person Specification for a teacher.

Organisations have two choices when seeking to recruit staff:

INTERNAL RECRUITMENT, where staff are promoted within the organisation.

EXTERNAL RECRUITMENT, where new staff are taken on.

INTERNAL RECRUITMENT

Advantages

- Internal recruitment can act as a motivator and can strengthen an employee's commitment to the organisation. This can reduce labour turnover and ensure that employees are working to their full potential.
- Current employees will have a working knowledge of the operation of the organisation and so they will not need to spend as much time being inducted.
- The organisation will have a good knowledge of the employees, which means that they

will know their capabilities; it is sometimes difficult to get an accurate picture of potential employees from their application form and interview performance.

- The internal recruitment process is quicker and less costly than external recruitment.
- If it recruits internally, there may be less disruption to the organisation.

Disadvantages

- If an employee has been promoted from within the organisation, this leaves their previous position vacant; it may be the case that external recruitment is still needed to fill this position.
- Current employees may be unable to bring fresh ideas to the organisation because they do not want to 'rock the boat' with colleagues, or they have insufficient experience outside the organisation. Ultimately, they may be too 'stuck in a rut' to think outside the box.
- There can be resentment within the organisation if several people have applied for the same position and only one person is appointed.
- Internal recruitment ignores potential employees from outside the organisation who may be better suited to the position.

EXTERNAL RECRUITMENT

Advantages

- External recruitment attracts a larger pool of potential applicants for a job and by degree a higher calibre of candidate.
- A new employee may be more willing to change working practices within an organisation as they have no previous links or allegiances to the existing staff.
- External employees should have wider experience if they have come from other organisations. This will allow them to introduce new ideas and methods of working to the organisation.

Disadvantages

- The recruitment of external candidates can be costly and time-consuming. There is a considerable time lag between the human resources department carrying out a job analysis and the time when an external candidate is actually recruited.
- Some people are very good at selling themselves at the interview stage of the recruitment process, yet in practice they may not be so good at carrying out the actual job. In this way, the most suitable candidate is not always recruited.
- It may take an external candidate time to settle into a new organisation and feel familiar with procedures. Sometimes though, this time is a luxury which the organisation cannot afford.
- If current employees do not see promotional prospects, they may become discontented and look for jobs outside the organisation. This will increase labour turnover within the organisation.

It is clear that both methods of recruitment have advantages and pitfalls, and the human resources department needs to consider each job vacancy in isolation. There may be a situation where a combination of both internal and external recruitment methods are used, depending upon individual circumstances. If the human resources department opts for external recruitment, there is a wide range of recruitment methods that they could consider.

TASK

Evaluate external versus internal methods of recruitment

METHODS OF EXTERNAL RECRUITMENT

Newspaper and magazine advertisements

This is perhaps the most common and widely used form of advertising for job vacancies. Depending on the nature of the job, either the local or national press will be used. Specialist vacancies or jobs requiring high levels of skill will usually be advertised nationally, whereas jobs requiring limited skills will be advertised locally. Specialist trade magazines or journals may also be used for very specialised job vacancies.

Department for Employment and Learning

This agency is a government-run agency and it advertises jobs in most major towns. Individuals are encouraged to apply for the advertised jobs and the agency organises interviews between the potential employer and employee.

Private employment agencies

These are organisations that specialise in recruitment and selection. Individuals register with the agency to try to get work and the agency tries to match its potential employees with employer requirements. The individuals will be interviewed by the agency, by the potential employers or by both. If successful in filling a vacancy, the agency will receive a commission from the employer. The major drawback of this approach is that they tend to provide staff who do not stay long in a particular job.

Headhunting

This involves a firm approaching an individual who is currently employed by another firm and offering them a position within their own organisation. The organisation will be seeking to attract someone who has a proven track record, although they may need to offer a considerable remuneration package if they are to tempt the individual to leave their existing job. Another major drawback with this approach is that there may be a lack of loyalty from the individual. If he/she left their previous company for money, there is the possibility that they may move on to another firm if they are given a new offer.

Visiting Universities – 'The Milk Round'

The Milk Round involves companies visiting universities around the UK, attempting to recruit graduates to their organisations. This is a fairly inexpensive method of recruitment, especially for large organisations. However, the interviewing process can be very time consuming as many candidates will need to be interviewed.

Once an organisation has decided to recruit externally, it must carefully consider the most appropriate method of recruitment.

TASK

Evaluate the different methods of recruitment available to an organisation.

SELECTION AND APPOINTMENT

Once the human resources department has identified the need to fill a vacancy, it must put in place a process for selection that is both fair to potential applicants and provides a valid framework for selecting suitable employees. Applicants should be chosen only on the basis of ability, skills and knowledge rather than on gender or race. Equal opportunities legislation has helped to ensure that firms adhere to these principles as it dictates the need for organisations to demonstrate that their recruitment procedures are fair. The job analysis, job descriptions, and person specifications all help to highlight the requirements that are needed for an individual position.

The department also needs to draw up application forms, outline how short lists should be drawn up, put in place procedures for interviews, and how to conduct tests if these are appropriate.

Application Forms

Application forms are the most common way of obtaining information about prospective candidates. They are a common template which applicants complete in order to be considered for a job. Application forms facilitate easy comparisons between candidates and allow the human resources department to decide whether potential candidates meet the criteria required for the position. Even though all application forms may be different, the following information is usually requested:

- Personal details such as name, address, and nationality
- Education and qualifications
- Hobbies and interests
- Past experience
- Reasons for wanting the job
- References

A Letter of Application

A letter of application is sometimes used instead of an application form. However, this method is not as common as it once was, as it is more difficult to compare candidates using this approach.

Curriculum Vitae

A curriculum vitae or CV is a detailed history of a candidate's qualifications, employment history, personal details and interests. It is sometimes requested in support of a letter of application or application form.

TASK

Using an application form of your choice, discuss the questions asked and why these might have been asked.

Interviews

Once the candidates (who meet the requirements of the position) are selected, the next stage of the recruitment process is usually the interview stage. The process of interviewing allows the human resources department to not only meet the candidate face to face but it also allows interviewees to expand on points that they have made on their application form. The major drawback of an interview is that some people do not perform well under interview conditions as they feel intimidated by the process. Furthermore, those people who interview well may not be capable of actually carrying out the duties required of the post. When conducting an interview, the human resources department should allow the candidate to 'sell themselves' and explain why they would make a good candidate for the position. Other guidelines include:

- Ensure that the information that is collected from the interview accurately predicts whether the candidate can perform the job.
- The human resources department should provide the candidate with adequate information about the job so they can answer the questions effectively.
- All candidates should be asked the same questions so that the interviewers can compare candidates more effectively.
- Questions should be fair so that all candidates can perform to the best of their ability.
- Questions should not be 'loaded' as this enables some individuals to perform better than others.

When conducting the interview, the human resources department will need to gain as much information from the candidate as possible. It has been suggested that interviews should obtain information from seven main areas.

INVESTING IN PEOPLE

Rodger's 7 Point Plan
• Physical Make Up
• Attainments
• General Intelligence
• Specialised Aptitude
• Interests
• Disposition
• Circumstances

TASK

Discuss why it is important to gain information about a candidate in each of these seven areas.

Despite the common use of interviewing as a recruitment technique, there are some arguments against using this as a method of selection.

- First impressions often dictate whether or not a candidate is chosen. As already discussed, some candidates have a natural flair for interviews but this does not mean they can actually do the job.

- In some cases the interviewers may have already decided upon the ideal candidate based on the application form.

- The interview process places more emphasis on the negative evidence presented rather than the positive.

TASK

Evaluate the use of interviewing in the recruitment process?

Testing

Many organisations now use testing as a method of selecting staff. Due to the drawbacks associated with interviews, some people argue that testing provides a more accurate way of predicting how a potential employee may perform in the workplace. Depending upon the type of job vacancy, there are different types of tests that can be carried out by the human resources department.

- Aptitude tests are tests that show how well a potential employee might handle a job-related problem or task.
- Attainment tests measure the level of skills that an employee has, such as how well they can type.
- Intelligence tests measure a candidate's general knowledge, numeracy skills and literacy skills.
- Personality/psychometric tests measure the characteristics and attitudes that an individual employee might have in relation to, for example, working with the general public.

TASK

To which types of jobs would each of the above tests be suited?

CASE STUDY

Research carried out in 2008 has shown that many human resources directors believe that interview questions, body language and intuition are not enough to detect the honesty of a candidate. In fact, research has shown that 57% of people think that it is acceptable to bend the truth in an interview.

In light of this, it is argued that psychometric testing (in conjunction with standard CVs and application forms) is an invaluable tool in identifying a candidate's abilities and competencies.

Contract of employment

Once a decision has been taken about who to appoint, the new member of staff should be given a contract of employment.

A contract of employment should include:

- Name of employer
- Name of employee
- Date the job commences
- Job title

- Place of work
- Rate of pay and frequency of payment
- Holiday arrangements
- Sickness benefits
- Grievance procedures
- Disciplinary procedures
- Period of notice required
- Pension arrangements

TRAINING

Staff training is essential to most organisations as it ensures that the firm can get the most out of its staff, while for employees, it provides opportunities for promotion and increased salary.

Benefits of training

- Training should result in a more productive workforce, which should help to improve the overall performance of the organisation.

- The workforce should be more flexible as they learn new skills.

- Accidents and injuries should be reduced.

- Training can help to improve the external image of a company.

- Employees should be more motivated if they believe that the organisation is investing in them.

However, training can be costly and organisations need to weigh up the financial and time implications against the benefits that will result.

Induction

Workers at all levels within an organisation need training and one of the first training activities that workers are exposed to is induction. Induction is usually a general introduction to the organisation and how it operates, rather than being job specific. It is intended to help the new employee adjust to the new work environment and to meet other employees who they will be working alongside. The induction process is an important activity for the human resources department as newly appointed employees are most likely to leave within the first few weeks of employment.

TRAINING REQUIREMENTS OF CURRENT STAFF

Training can take place either on-the-job or off-the-job. On-the-job training takes place at the employee's workplace, whereas off-the-job training takes place away from the workplace.

On-the-job training

On-the-job training can be carried out in many different ways, some of which include being trained or 'shown the ropes' by an experienced fellow worker. Employees may also be mentored or coached by experienced workers.

Advantages
- On-the-job training is a relatively cheap method of training.
- The trainee does not need to take time off as the training is happening in the workplace.

Disadvantages
- The human resources department needs to be careful that it selects a suitable employee to carry out the training.
- The experienced employee may neglect his/her own job whilst carrying out training, which can be costly to the organisation.
- The trainee might make mistakes, which could be costly for the organisation.

Off-the-job training

Off-the-job training occurs when an employee attends a course. This can take place in many different ways, such as taking external vocational courses at a local further education college. Distance learning or e-learning has become a common way for employees to receive off-the-job training.

Advantages
- Employees should be properly trained as the courses are run by experienced instructors.
- The trainee can learn at his/her own pace.
- The costs of training are easy to calculate.
- In some situations the employee can receive a formal qualification.

Disadvantages
- Off-the-job training is more expensive than on-the-job training.
- The learning is not taking place in the environment where the employee will be utilising the skills and knowledge.
- The equipment used in off-the-job training may differ from that used in the workplace.

TASK

Evaluate on-the-job and off-the-job training.

METHODS OF TRAINING

There is a range of training methods available to organisations and each has advantages and disadvantages.

Presentation or lecture

Advantages
- This method allows trainers to easily control the time spent on training.
- A presentation or lecture is useful for a large group.

Disadvantages
- This method can be quite dull if used without learner participation.
- Interaction amongst participants is limited.

Structured exercise or role play

Advantages
- This method allows trainers to practice new skills in a controlled environment.
- Learners are actually involved in the training.

Disadvantages
- The trainer needs time to prepare for such a session.
- It can be difficult for the trainer to tailor all learners' situations.

Individual reading, assignments and exercises

Advantages
- This method saves time.
- Material can be retained for later use.

Disadvantages
- This method can become boring if it is used too long.
- Learners read at different speeds.

Facilitated group discussion

Advantages
- This method keeps learners interested and involved.
- Learner resources can be shared.
- Learning can be observed.

Disadvantages
- This method can make it difficult for trainers to control the time spent on training.
- Learning can become confusing.
- Some learners may dominate the group.

TASK

Evaluate methods of training available to an organisation of your choice.

CASE STUDY

Research carried out by Manpower Employment Agency in 2008 has shown that 80% of employees expect their employers to provide work-based learning. The study also found that 67% would consider changing jobs if the training was not provided. Against this, only 39% of employees reported that they received formal training in their jobs.

APPRAISAL

Once an employee has been working in an organisation, the firm may carry out an appraisal. This helps the organisation to find out about the qualities of the employee and to assess how the employee is performing. The results of the appraisal can be used as a way of identifying training needs and possible promotional opportunities. The appraisal is also a useful forum for agreeing job objectives and motivating an employee.

CCEA SPECIMEN QUESTION - SUMMER 07 AS 2

Study the information below and answer the questions that follow.

Recruitment Process

Technico plc is a Belfast based company currently employing 300 workers. It manufactures a range of consumer electrical products, mainly for the UK market. As part of its expansion strategy, Technico plc intends to significantly extend its product range over the next two years. However, to do so, it will need to recruit 10 scientists to work in its research and development department.

Robert Shaw, the human resources manager, has already taken the decision to recruit these workers externally. He reasoned that any internal training process would take too long. External recruitment would be quicker because less training would be needed and it would bring fresh ideas into the business. Technico plc is prepared to offer suitable applicants a highly competitive salary combined with excellent conditions of service.

Robert now needs to choose appropriate methods of external recruitment and selection. Although it would be possible to fill the vacancies using only graduates from local universities, Robert realises that Technico plc needs to achieve a good balance of applicants. He wants to ensure that Technico plc employs scientists with appropriate industrial experience as well as relevant academic qualifications. Such a combination will contribute towards giving Technico plc a competitive advantage over its rivals.

(a) Explain three methods of external recruitment that Technico plc could use in this situation. [10]

(b) Discuss the selection methods that Technico plc might use to ensure that suitable workers are recruited. [15]

CCEA SPECIMEN QUESTION - JAN 07 AS 2

Study the information below and answer the questions that follow.

Induction and Health and Safety

John Armstrong is the Managing Director of Alljob Ltd, an engineering firm employing forty workers. Although the business has been performing well over the past few years, the recent retirement of a senior salesperson has led to a fall in orders. This, in turn, has caused cash flow problems within the business.

John has been made aware of another problem which may worsen these cash flow difficulties. It started two weeks ago when a new worker was being shown around the factory as part of his induction programme. Unfortunately, he fell down an uneven staircase and broke his arm. Following that, a secretary narrowly missed being hit by a slate falling from the roof as she arrived for work. These incidents caused many of the other workers to become concerned about health and safety in the workplace. A trade union representative investigated the issues and presented John with a long list of measures that, he claimed, needed to be implemented in order to make Alljob Ltd a safe place to work.

John is concerned about the recent incidents but knows that the measures suggested will be very expensive to implement. He considers that many of the items on the list are not really necessary. However, the trade union representative insists that John must meet the requirements of the Health and Safety at Work (NI) Order 1978.

(a) Explain three reasons why Alljob Ltd should have an induction programme for new workers. [10]

Chapter 6:   BREAKEVEN ANALYSIS

6

The breakeven point is the point at which a firm neither makes a profit nor a loss. This analysis is important for an organisation as it will indicate how many units of a product or service are needed for the firm to break even.

Before the breakeven point can be calculated, it is necessary to understand the difference between fixed costs and variable costs.

FIXED COSTS: These are costs that remain the same irrespective of output levels. Examples would include rent, rates, and salaries. Graphically, they are represented by a horizontal line, reinforcing the fact that the costs do not change as output changes.

VARIABLE COSTS: These are costs that change as output levels change. Examples would include raw materials, direct labour, and electricity. Graphically, they are represented by a diagonal line that cuts the origin, showing the costs increasing as output levels rise.

SEMI-VARIABLE COSTS

Some costs cannot readily be classified as a fixed cost or a variable cost and are classified as semi-variable costs. An example of a semi-variable cost would be a telephone bill, which is made up of two different types of charges. Part of the bill is for line rental, which is fixed for the period in question. The other part of the bill is the charge for the number of calls made. Therefore, the telephone bill has an element of fixed cost associated with it and an element of variable cost.

BREAKEVEN ANALYSIS

TOTAL COSTS: These are Fixed Costs + Variable Costs. Again, these are represented by a diagonal line except the line cuts the **y** axis (costs) at the same point as the fixed cost line. This is because at the point where there is no output, fixed costs will still need to be paid.

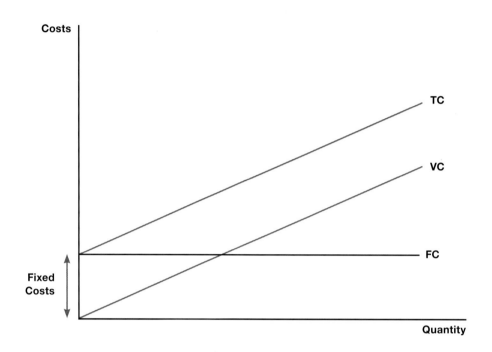

A vital aspect of any business is to see what output level or sales level is necessary before it breaks even. However, breakeven does not specify the time that it will take to reach this level. This will depend on how quickly sales are generated and in some cases it can be many years before a firm will reach its breakeven sales level. To work out breakeven, it is essential to know the following information:

1.   The price being charged
2.   The variable costs
3.   The fixed costs

From this information, the breakeven level of output can be calculated.

Example
Price = £5
Variable costs = £3 per unit
Fixed costs = £2,000

From this information, every time one unit is sold there is an excess of income over variable costs of £2. This figure is called the **contribution.**

Contribution = Selling price per unit – Variable cost per unit

However, this is **NOT** the same as profit, because the fixed costs of £1,000 also have to be paid. It is therefore necessary to work out how many units need to be sold for the total contribution to be equal to the fixed costs. In this case, the contribution is £2 per unit and the fixed costs are £2,000, so if we can sell 1,000 units then we will have had enough contribution to pay the fixed costs. Any units we sell beyond that level will then make a profit of £2 each. So if we sell 1,001 units, our total profit will be £2. If we sell 1,002 units, our total profit will be £4 etc.

The breakeven level of output can therefore be calculated from the following formula:

$$\textbf{Breakeven output} = \frac{\textbf{Fixed costs}}{\textbf{Contribution (per unit)}}$$

The breakeven level of information can also be obtained by plotting the figures on a graph. To do this the following steps need to be followed:

Stage 1

Calculate the break even point using the above formula. This will allow us to make decisions regarding the scale to be used for the graph.

Stage 2

Multiply the breakeven point in units by 2. This will give us an indication as to how many units we need to represent on the graph. The units are represented along the x axis (horizontal). Plot the number of units along the x axis up to approximately twice the breakeven amount of units.

Stage 3

This stage often causes the most problems as there is the temptation to draw the y axis and simply divide it into even numbers. If we are to be accurate when deciding on an appropriate axis, the costs and revenues on this axis must correspond with the number of units along the x axis.

One way of doing this is to draw a diagonal line that cuts the origin in two. This 45% line is the firm's total revenue line. If we read along the x axis we can read off what the corresponding revenues should be on the y axis.

For example, if we are selling each unit of production for £30 and we are producing 10 units, then we should read across from the total revenue line at 10 units, and the point on the y axis should be £300. We can continue to do this until the scale on the **y** axis is complete.

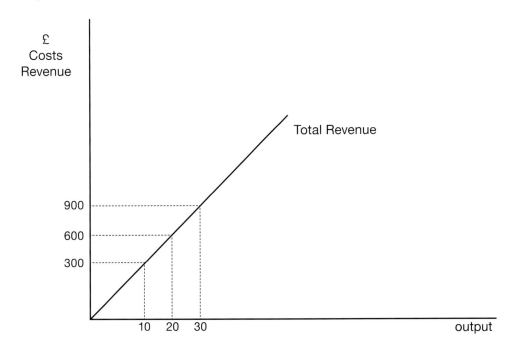

BREAKEVEN ANALYSIS

Stage 4

Now that we have the scales correct on the graph and we have the total revenue line plotted, the next step is to draw the fixed cost line. As already discussed, the fixed cost line is horizontal since costs will not change as levels of output change.

Stage 5

The next stage involves drawing the firm's total cost line.

In order to draw a straight line on a graph, it is useful to remember that we only need to know two points. We have already discussed the properties of the firm's fixed cost line so we know that it starts where the fixed cost line cuts the y axis. (Fixed costs still need to be paid when no production is taking place; therefore, total costs are equal to fixed costs when output is zero.)

The second point that we can plot is the breakeven point. We have calculated this using the formula. The breakeven point in units can therefore be plotted on the graph where it cuts the firm's total revenue line. This is the second point that we need to plot on the total cost curve because by definition, breakeven is the point where total revenue and total costs are equal.

We can now highlight the area of profit and loss on the graph. If you are confused, the area of profit is where total revenue is above total costs and the area of loss is where total cost is above total revenue.

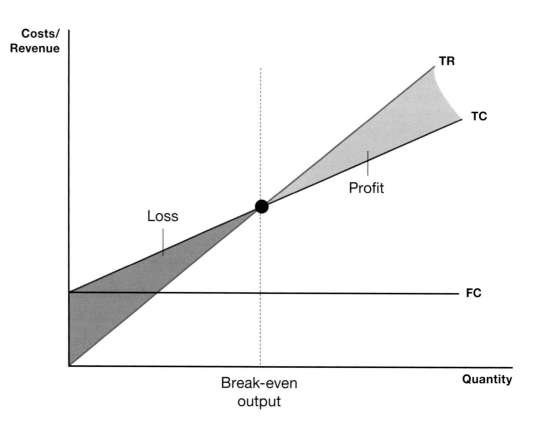

Stage 6

The margin of safety of the firm can also be illustrated on the graph. The margin of safety shows how far from breakeven output the firm is currently producing. It shows, in other words, how much output could fall before the firm started making a loss. The margin of safety is shown on the diagram below:

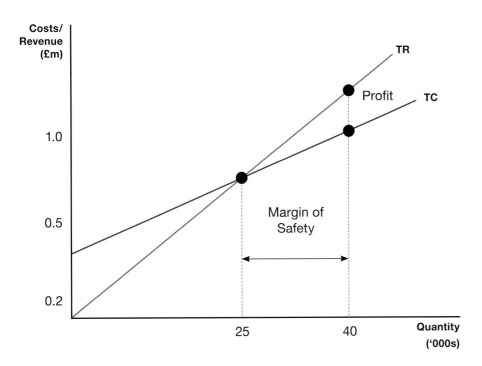

Margin of safety can also be calculated using the formula below. This formula shows the percentage of sales that a firm is making over and above its breakeven point.

EXISTING OR EXPECTED SALES – BREAKEVEN SALES × 100

EXISTING OR EXPECTED SALES × 1

Organisation can also use break even analysis as a way of calculating the output required to earn a target level of profit. (This can be calculated by using formulae 2 on the next page.)

LIMITATIONS

Despite the usefulness of breakeven analysis, there are some limitations.

- Breakeven analysis tells us nothing about what sales are actually likely to be for the product. This is an important limitation as it does not take into consideration what the demand for the product might be.
- It assumes that fixed costs (FC) are constant. This may not always be the case as economies of scale may arise.
- It assumes average variable costs are constant per unit of output, at least in the range of likely quantities of sales. Again these may change as output levels change.
- It assumes that the quantity of goods produced is equal to the quantity of goods sold.
- As already identified, it is sometimes difficult to classify costs as either fixed or variable. Some costs are semi-variable.

BREAKEVEN ANALYSIS

TASK

Evaluate break even analysis as a decision making tool.

USEFUL BREAKEVEN ANALYSIS FORMULAE

1. Breakeven in units

$$\frac{\text{FIXED COSTS}}{\text{CONTRIBUTION PER UNIT}}$$

2. Breakeven in sales   (£££)

$$\frac{\text{FIXED COSTS}}{\text{CONTRIBUTION PER UNIT}} \times \text{SALES PRICE PER UNIT}$$

3. To earn a target profit in units

$$\frac{\text{FIXED COST + TARGET PROFIT}}{\text{CONTRIBUTION PER UNIT}}$$

4. To earn a target profit in sales (££££)

$$\frac{\text{FIXED COSTS + TARGET PROFIT}}{\text{CONTRIBUTION PER UNIT}} \times \text{SALES PRICE PER UNIT}$$

MARGIN OF SAFETY

The percentage of existing or expected sales that may decrease before the company incurs a loss.

$$\frac{\text{EXISTING OR EXPECTED SALES – BREAKEVEN SALES}}{\text{EXISTING OR EXPECTED SALES}} \times \frac{100}{1}$$

Review Questions

1 A factory has the capacity to produce 400,000 litres of shampoo per month. The shampoo sells for £2.00 per unit; the variable costs are £1.20 per unit. The company's fixed costs are £140,000 per month. Existing sales are 300,000 litres per month.

(a) Calculate the breakeven in units and sales.

(b) What level of sales is required to make a profit of £120,000 per month?

(c) If variable costs increase by 5%, what level of sales will be required to break even?

(d) Calculate the margin of safety for the factory.

BREAKEVEN ANALYSIS

2. The Hard Stuff Company can produce 400,000 litres of a new non-alcoholic cocktail per month. The selling price is estimated at £4.00 per litre; the variable costs are estimated at £2.40 per month. The fixed costs are £144,000. Assume existing sales are £500,000.

   (a) Calculate the breakeven in units, and in sales.
   (b) Calculate what levels of sales are needed to make a profit of £270,000 per month.

3. A toy manufacturer can sell all the toys he produces. The selling price of each toy is £25; the variable costs are £10.00. The fixed costs of running the business are £4,500 each month.

   (a) How many toys need to be sold each month for the business to break even?
   (b) Current production is 400 toys each month. What is the profit?

4. The Irish Bakery can produce 500,000 loaves of bread. The loaves sell for £3.00 as they are organic. The variable costs are £1.50 per unit. The fixed costs are £450,000. Calculate the breakeven in sales, units, and the level of sales that are required to make a profit of £500,000. Calculate the margin of safety, and draw a traditional breakeven graph. Assume existing sales are £1m.

5. (a) Define the term breakeven.

   (b) A pizza parlour currently produces 5,000 pizzas a week. The selling price of the pizzas is £2.45; the variable costs are £1.50. The fixed costs are £2,750.

   i) Calculate the breakeven in units and sales for this pizza parlour.
   ii) What is the margin of safety?
   iii) How many pizzas would the parlour have to bake to earn a profit of £10,000?
   iv) Draw a traditional breakeven graph.

   (c) If the variable costs were £1.75, how many pizzas would the company have to manufacture to breakeven?

6. (a) What is meant by the margin of safety?

   (b) The Hotels Friend is a professional laundry company. It launders 20,000 sheets a week. The company charges £1.15 for every sheet laundered. Max, the manager, estimates that the variable costs are £0.57; the fixed costs are £7,400. Calculate the breakeven in sales, and how many sheets the company would have to launder to make a profit of £25,000.

   (c) If Max increases the charge per sheet to £1.60, how many sheets would he have to launder to break even? Calculate the breakeven from a traditional breakeven chart.

7. The Winery manufactures wine racks that sell for £5.40 each. The variable costs are £3.00, and the fixed costs are £1,400 a month. The company currently sells 1,200 racks a month. Calculate the company's breakeven in units, the company's margin of safety, and how many racks it would need to sell to make a profit of £7,000. Draw a traditional breakeven chart for the company.

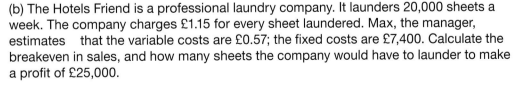
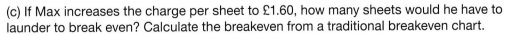

Chapter 7: BUDGETS

A budget is a plan that is drawn up setting out revenues or costs (or both) for a given period of time. Most budgets are drawn up for the financial year and are usually broken down into shorter time periods such as months. The budget allows comparisons to be made between actual results and what was budgeted and to assess how an organisation has been performing. The differences between the two figures are known as variances and these can be either adverse or favourable. Budgets are therefore a useful tool which help an organisation become more effective.

THE BUDGETARY CONTROL PROCESS

Although budgets are expressed in monetary terms – showing the income and expenditure needed during a financial period – they may be initially calculated using quantities such as labour hours or kilograms of materials. Budgets are drawn up for individual departments and functional areas, and are inter-related.

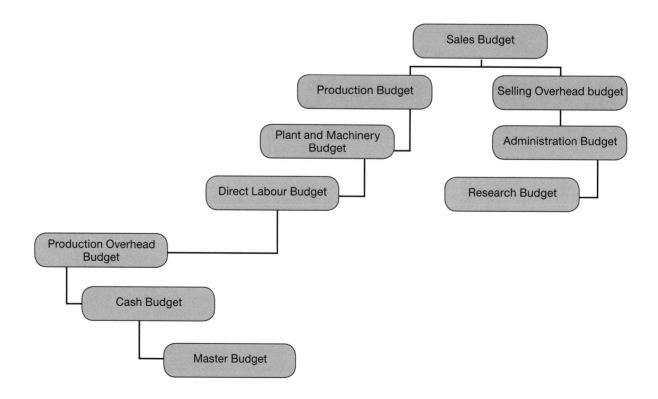

INTER-RELATIONSHIPS OF BUDGETS

Example

Zee Mobile Ltd produces mobile telephones. The sales director has estimated that the following quantities will be sold in the next six months.

	Jan	Feb	Mar	Apr	May	Jun
Sales	2,000	2,400	3,000	3,200	3,200	3,500

The production department will manufacture these telephones in the month before the sales take place and it has been agreed to maintain a stock of 400 telephones at any one time. On 1 December this stock was 200 telephones.

The first step that management should take is to draw up a table providing all this information.

	Dec	Jan	Feb	Mar	Apr	May	Jun
Opening Stock	200	2,400	2,800	3,400	3,600	3,600	3,900
Production	2,200	2,400	3,000	3,200	3,200	3,500	
Sales		2,000	2,400	3,000	3,200	3,200	1,750
Closing Stock	2,400	2,800	3,400	3,600	3,600	3,900	

This table clearly shows how many mobile telephones need to be produced each month. Once this information has been calculated, management will need to make decisions, always conscious of how changes to the production budget will impact on other departmental budgets. One of the first decisions is to assess whether the organisation has the capacity to produce these mobile telephones; the machine capacity of the organisation will need to be evaluated as too will the company's current labour situation.

The reason for assessing these factors is that more machines and labour may be required, especially in the busier months. If this is the case, the budgets associated with these areas will be affected and the accountant will need to look at any cash requirements to meet these changes. These changes will be reflected in the cash budget. Therefore, a change in one budget will impact those of other departments.

When drawing up budgets, there are different approaches that may be adopted. A 'top-down' approach to budget-setting would involve the owners or directors of an organisation deciding on the individual plans for each department, and these plans are then given to the individual managers to implement.

BUDGETS

Other organisations prefer a 'bottom up' approach where individual managers draw up their own budgets, and these are given to the owners or directors who coordinate the individual budgets into a master budget. In such a case, a budget committee may be formed, made up of all the functional or departmental managers. The committee reviews the budgets submitted by individual managers and there may need to be negotiations between the functional areas to introduce budget changes.

There are a number of different types of budgets. A **fixed budget** is not changed, even when the actual activity levels differ from those set. A **flexible budget** is one which is changed to allow for the behaviour of variable costs at different levels of activity. Additionally, budgets can be classified as incremental budgets (also known as historic budgets) or zero-based budgets.

Incremental budgeting simply involves taking the previous year's budget figures and adding on percentage increases, either for inflation, or where circumstances demand it.

Zero-based budgeting is often used in a new or unstable business. Each time a new budget is drawn up, it is not based on the previous year but is based on entirely new costings and projections.

Benefits of budgeting

- Budgeting allows an organisation to control both its income and expenditure and can highlight areas where the organisation is not performing as efficiently as it could. It is therefore a useful control mechanism for the business.
- Budgets are a useful way of clarifying the roles and responsibilities of management within an organisation.
- Budgets help to coordinate the activities of an organisation and can improve the communication between departments.
- Budgets help to ensure that scarce resources are used as efficiently as possible.
- Performance can be measured against set targets.
- Budgets can help to motivate employees.

Disadvantages of budgeting

- Budgeting is dependent on the quality of the information provided. Poor quality information results in budgets that are meaningless.
- Budgets can become very inflexible.
- Budgets can be demotivating if the users have not been involved in the budgeting process.
- There can be a danger of management becoming over dependent on budgets at the expense of managing.

TASK

Evaluate budgeting as a tool for management.

CASH BUDGETS

All of the main budgets contribute to the firm's cash budget which in turn provides the data for the master budget (ie the forecasted financial statements). The cash budget is therefore central to all organisations.
Cash Budgets (also known as a Cash-flow forecast) are drawn up to outline the expected cash/bank receipts and payments for a business, usually on a month by month basis. A balance is shown each month and this allows the business to forecast periods when outgoings are higher than incomings.

A Cash Budget may be defined as *'a forecast of receipts and payments which is normally prepared on a monthly basis for the budget period'*.

It is not sufficient to make a profit. Managers must also ensure that the business has adequate cash because one of the main causes of bankruptcy is poor cash management.

The two main elements of the cash budget are the **forecasts** and the **timing** of funds.

Receipts are any items of cash received. Payments are any items paid for in cash. The cash budget for a month, a quarter, or a year, will only include items that affect the company's cash/bank balance.

The following table shows some typical receipts and payments:

RECEIPTS	PAYMENTS
Cash Receipts	Payment for purchases
Debtor Receipts	Overheads
Interest Received	Tax
Tax refund	Drawings

Items that are not included in the cash budget
Depreciation is not included in a cash budget. This is because no cash payment is ever made for depreciation.

Uses of a cash budget

Cash budgets are drawn up for various reasons:

- Management can forecast cash balances, and identify any cash shortages or cash surpluses.
- Cash budgets are forecasts and enable management to easily ask 'what if' questions, eg if we had to pay creditors within 3 weeks, how would it impact cash flow etc?
- If a cash budget reveals that a large bank overdraft is required, the company may then consider revising its budgeted projections.

BUDGETS

1. THE DIFFERENCE BETWEEN CASH AND PROFIT

The trading profit and loss account focuses on the profit or gain after all expenses have been paid. The cash budget focuses on managing the cash flow in a business.

The closing cash balance for any month is not the same as the net profit for the month. It is a forecast of the cash or money available to pay suppliers and wages.

2. THE TIMING OF RECEIPTS AND PAYMENTS

The cash budget is concerned with the **timing** of **cash** receipts and payments. For example, in January, the sales figures were £1,000, and the sales receipts were £1,500. Why might this be the case?

Similarly, purchases for January were £900, and the payments for purchases were £600. Why was this?

Worked example

Sales for January were £5,000; 20% of this was cash sales and 80% was paid for one month later.

The timing of the receipts was as follows:
Jan.   £1,000
Feb.   £4,000

TASK

How would the following transactions be recorded?

1. Sales for February were £10,000; 15% of this was cash sales and the remainder was received two months later.

2. Purchases for March were £5,000; 50% of these must be paid for in cash, the remainder is paid for one month later.

3. Sales for January were £3,500; 10% of this was cash sales, 20% was received one month later and the remainder was received two months later.

4. Purchases for February were £8,000; 5% of this was paid for up front, 10% was paid for one month later and the balance was paid for two months later.

5. In January, Bob had sales of £15,000; 40% of these were paid in cash and the balance was paid for one month later. (Bob is also due money from sales in December, which were £10,000. 50% of this sum is due to be received one month later.)

3. PREPARING A CASH BUDGET

(Steps 1 and 2 are the planning or rough work stages. Attention to these should make step 3 a lot easier to complete.)

1. Prepare a sales schedule

(This is a plan of the monthly sales and then monthly receipts.)

2. Prepare a purchases schedule

(This is a plan of monthly purchases and then monthly payments for purchases.)

3. Prepare the actual cash budget

The normal headings for a cash budget are:

Title	Jan	Feb	Mar	
Receipts *eg debtors*				
Total receipts				
Payments *eg drawings*				
Total Payments				
Receipts-Payments				
Opening Bank Balance				
Closing Bank Balance				

Worked example:

BBA				
Cash Budget for BBA Limited for June, July, August				
	June	July	August	
RECEIPTS				
Cash Sales	7,000	6,000	5,000	
Debtors	54,000	45,000	63,000	
TOTAL RECEIPTS	61,000	51,000	68,000	

BUDGETS

PAYMENTS				
Purchases	30,000	25,000	35,000	
Wages	12,000	10,000	9,000	
Overheads	12,000	16,000	14,000	
Commission	2,250	3,150	2,700	
Loan repayment	25,000			
Machine		15,000	15,000	
TOTAL PAYMENTS	81,250	69,150	75,700	
Receipts less Payments	-20,250	-18,150	-7,700	
O. Bank Bal	22,000	1,750	-16,400	
C. Bank Bal	1,750	-16,400	-24,100	

It is important to note that in this example the business had an opening bank balance of £22,000.

It should also be noted that the closing bank balance of one month becomes the opening bank balance of the next month.

4. MANAGING CASH DEFICITS

It is not enough to identify cash deficits; managers must know how to manage situations where cash deficits may arise. There are many solutions to managing cash deficits, some of which include the following:

- Leasing instead of buying equipment
- Delaying the purchase of equipment
- Shortening the average debtor collection period
- Reducing stock levels
- Asking suppliers to extend credit periods

TASK

Evaluate the advantages and disadvantages of these solutions for managing cash deficits.

VARIANCE ANALYSIS

The main benefit of the budgeting process is that it allows management to compare the actual performance of an organisation with what had been budgeted. The process allows users to identify situations where differences may have arisen.

Differences between actual and budgeted performance are known as variances, and are either favourable or adverse. A favourable variance arises if the actual performance is better than what was budgeted, whereas an adverse variance occurs if the actual performance is worse.

Variances can arise as a result of many different factors, including:

- **Random deviations** – In some cases variances can be outside the control of the manager such as the depreciation of a computer. In such instances, management cannot be held responsible for an adverse variance occurring.

- **Budgets set incorrectly** – Sometimes the actual budget itself may have been set incorrectly. Management may, for example, have been too ambitious in relation to what they thought they could achieve.

- **Failure to meet agreed budgets** – some managers may simply ignore the budget that was set, resulting in variances occurring.

Budgeting and the associated variance analysis process are advantageous as they provide management with a useful control mechanism. However, despite this, there are certain limitations associated with their use.

The process can be quite rigid, and there is often little flexibility for managers to deviate from the set budget if required. For example, due to unforeseen circumstances, an organisation may be faced with a downturn in sales. A manager may feel that additional advertising is needed, but this may not have been identified in the budget. The manager will therefore be faced with the dilemma of ignoring the budget in an attempt to increase sales, or may decide to stick with the budget at the expense of increasing sales.

We will now look at some actual budgets and explain how variances may arise.

Sales variances

Sales Variance = Actual sales – Budgeted sales

A favourable variance will arise if actual sales turn out to be better than what had been budgeted. However, an adverse variance will occur when actual sales are not as high as budgeted.

It is not enough to identify a sales variance – management must know how to take corrective action to rectify the situation. For instance, if there is an adverse sales variance, management may need to look at factors such as the pricing of products, reasons for any changes in demand, and the marketing of their products.

BUDGETS

Materials variances

Materials Variance = Budgeted cost of materials – Actual cost of materials

A favourable materials variance will occur if costs are less than budgeted, whereas an adverse materials budget will arise if costs are higher than budgeted. In these situations the manager will look at factors such as whether the cost of materials has changed, or if the quantities of materials used have changed.

Labour variances

Labour Variance = Budgeted cost of labour – Actual cost of labour

In this situation a variance will be favourable if the actual cost of labour is lower than that budgeted; if the actual cost is higher than that budgeted, an adverse variance will occur. Management will need to look at the number of labour hours worked and the wages paid when examining this variance.

Overhead variances

Overhead Variance = Budgeted cost of overheads – Actual cost of overheads

A favourable overhead variance will arise if the actual cost of overheads is less than the budgeted cost of overheads, while with an adverse variance the actual cost of overheads is greater than that budgeted. There is a range of overheads that management can assess if a variance occurs, such as rent, rates, electricity etc.

Worked example

Complete the budget statement below, highlighting whether the variances are favourable or adverse:

	Actual Results £ 000's	Budgeted Results £ 000's	Variance	Favourable or Adverse
Direct Materials	120	130		
Labour	90	80		
Administration Overheads	30	25		
Fixed Overheads	80	85		
Total Costs				
Total Sales	450	430		
Profit				

Note: Profit has been calculated by subtracting total costs from total sales.

Examples:

1

Investigate the following cost figures for a manufacturing company:

	Budgeted Cost £	Actual Cost £
Materials	60,000	55,000
Labour	100,000	120,000
Overheads	25,000	24,000
Total Cost	185,000	199,000

(a) Calculate the variances for each cost.

(b) Identify if they are adverse or favourable.

(c) Suggest some factors which might have caused each of the variances.

2

(a) Complete the budget statement below, highlighting whether the variances are favourable or adverse:

	Actual Results £ 000's	Budgeted Results £ 000's	Variance	Favourable or Adverse
Direct Materials	55	65		
Labour	33	45		
Administration Overheads	65	75		
Fixed Overheads	100	100		
Total Costs				
Total Sales	380	360		
Profit				

(b) Make suggestions as to what might have caused the variances in each case.

(c) What action could you take to reverse any of the adverse variances?

3

(a) Complete the budget statement below, highlighting whether the variances are favourable or adverse:

	Actual Results £ 000's	Budgeted Results £ 000's	Variance	Favourable or Adverse
Direct Materials	100	80		
Labour	45	55		
Administration Overheads	22	28		
Fixed Overheads	120	100		
Total Costs				
Total Sales	510	530		
Profit				

3..

(b) Make suggestions as to what might have caused the variances in each case.

(c) What action could you take to reverse any of the adverse variances?

4

(a) Complete the budget statement below, highlighting whether the variances are favourable or adverse:

	Actual Results £ 000's	Budgeted Results £ 000's	Variance	Favourable or Adverse
Direct Materials	90	80		
Labour	65	55		
Administration Overheads	44	25		
Fixed Overheads	180	190		
Total Costs				
Total Sales	650	630		
Profit				

(b) Make suggestions as to what might have caused the variances in each case.

(c) What action could you take to reverse any of the adverse variances?

CCEA SPECIMEN QUESTION - SUMMER 07 AS 2

Study the information below and answer the questions that follow.

Variance Analysis

Botlit Ltd is a family owned company which manufactures plastic bottles for soft drinks producers. In recent years the business has lost sales to foreign competitors who have been quicker to adopt modern production techniques. Eric Lobbet, the founder and managing director of Botlit Ltd, realised that the situation had to be addressed. He asked the financial manager to devise a strategy to reduce the costs of the company.

The first stage in this strategy has just been completed. This involved the introduction of a computerised information network. It enabled managers at all levels within the firm to access up-to-date, accurate data relating to production and sales. Eric sees this as essential for the second stage of the strategy, the introduction of a variance analysis system.

Unfortunately, there is a good deal of opposition to this plan. Managers have had to implement many changes over the last two years and the introduction of variance analysis is viewed with deep suspicion amongst the workforce. The financial manager decides to demonstrate to other managers how this system might help Botlit Ltd and produces actual and budgeted figures for the last month. These are shown in **Table 1** (on page 89). Some of the figures are missing.

CCEA SPECIMEN QUESTION - SUMMER 07 AS 2

Table 1
Budgeted and Actual performance of Botlit Ltd: May 2007

	Budgeted	Actual	Variance	Adverse/Favourable
Sales revenue	£900,000	£800,000	?	?
Electricity costs	£16,000	£16,500	?	?
Cost of raw materials	£750,000	£730,000	£20,000	Favourable

(a) (i) Calculate the following variances and state whether each is adverse or favourable:

- The sales revenue variance
- The electricity costs variance [4]

(ii) Explain three factors that might have caused the sales revenue variance shown in Table 1. [6]

(b) Discuss the impact on Botlit Ltd of introducing a system of variance analysis. [15]

Chapter 8: FINAL ACCOUNTS

A sole trader is an individual trading in his or her name, or under a suitable trading name. A sole trader is the most common form of business. Out of approximately 3.6 million businesses in the United Kingdom, over 2 million are sole traders.

Each year a business will draw up its final accounts. These accounts show the profits that a business has made and will list the business' assets and liabilities. These accounts are drawn up from a trial balance.

THE TRIAL BALANCE

The trial balance is drawn up by the business' bookkeeper, who adds up all of the balances of its debtors and creditors' accounts. Some of these accounts will include sales accounts, purchases accounts, expenses accounts, creditors' accounts, and debtors' accounts.

The trial balance is a list of balances, arranged in two columns according to whether they are debit balances or credit balances. When all of the balances are entered they are totalled and both columns should be the same.

Example
Trial Balance, 31 December 2008

	Dr	Cr
	£	£
Bank	9,350	
Capital		15,000
Purchases	870	
Sales		475
Motor Van	4,950	
Debtors	220	
Drawings	185	
Creditors		275
Insurance	175	
	15,750	**15,750**

THE TRADING ACCOUNT

Once the trial balance is drawn up it will be handed to the accountant who will prepare the final accounts of the business. These are known as final accounts because they are produced at the end of the financial year for the business.

The final accounts are made up of the Trading/Profit and Loss Account, and the Balance Sheet.

The trading/profit and loss account may be subdivided into the trading account and the profit and loss account.

The trading account sets out the **gross profit** that the business has made, and the profit and loss account sets out the **net profit** that has been made.

Gross profit is what the business has gained from trading (buying and selling). It is calculated by taking the difference between the firm's sales and the cost of goods sold.

Gross Profit = Sales – Cost of Goods Sold

Cost of goods sold is calculated by adding Opening Stock (the stock that the firm has at the beginning of the trading period) to purchases, and subtracting Closing Stock (the stock left over at the end of the trading period).

Cost of Goods Sold = Opening Stock + Purchases – Closing Stock

Example

Joe has been given a box of 48 Mars Bars by his uncle. Unfortunately Joe does not like Mars Bars so he decides to sell them at a local car boot sale.

At the sale he is offered another box of 48 bars at a knock down price. He now has 96 bars. During the sale he sells 20 bars, leaving him with 76 bars.

OPENING STOCK	48	
ADD PURCHASES	48	96
LESS CLOSING STOCK		76
GOODS SOLD		20

If Joe values the Mars bars at 30 pence each, his accounts would be as follows:

	£	£		
OPENING STOCK	14.40			(48 × 30p)
ADD PURCHASES	14.40	28.80		(48 × 30p)
LESS CLOSING STOCK		22.80		(76 × 30p)
COST OF GOODS SOLD			6.00	(20 × 30p)

FINAL ACCOUNTS

Trading Account of Happy Burgers Ltd For Year Ending 31 December 2008

	£	£	£
Sales			500,000
Opening Stock	6,000		
Purchases	256,000	262,000	
Closing Stock		10,000	
Cost of Goods Sold			252,000
Gross Profit			248,000

It is important to note that sales and purchases only include items that are bought and sold during normal trading. They do not include items such as machinery or vehicles. These are classified as Fixed Assets.

PROFIT AND LOSS ACCOUNT

This account subtracts any expenses that have been incurred from the gross profit figure to give Net Profit.

Net Profit = Gross Profit – Expenses

The profit and loss account looks at how well the firm has traded over the time period concerned (usually the last six months or year). It basically shows how much the firm has earned from selling its product or service, and how much it has paid out in costs (production costs, salaries etc). The difference between these two is the amount of profit that has been earned.

Profit and Loss Account of Happy Burgers Ltd For Year Ending 31 December 2008

	£	£	£
Gross Profit			248,000
Less Expenses			
Wages and Salaries		55,000	
Electricity		34,000	
Rent and Rates		10,000	99,000
Net Profit			149,000

It is normal practice to combine the trading account and the profit and loss account into a single format.

Trading and Profit and Loss Account of Happy Burgers Ltd For Year Ending 31 December 2008

	£	£	£
Sales			500,000
Opening Stock	6,000		
Purchases	256,000	262,000	
Closing Stock		10,000	
Cost of Goods Sold			252,000
Gross Profit			248,000
Less Expenses			
Wages and Salaries		55,000	
Electricity		34,000	
Rent and Rates		10,000	99,000
Net Profit			149,000

Before examining the layout of the balance sheet, it is important to examine some of the accounting terms associated with it.

ASSETS

Assets are items which are owned by a business or money which is owed to the business. Assets fall into two groups:

Fixed Assets. These are items that have a life span of more than one year. They are usually items that the business expects to keep. Fixed assets include land and buildings, plant and machinery, fixtures and fittings, and motor vehicles. These assets are fixed because they are necessary for the business to trade but are not affected by the level of trade or the profit made. If a business purchases any fixed assets, then this is known as capital expenditure.

Current Assets. These are items which are much shorter term. The value of these items change in proportion to the amount of trade conducted by the business. Current assets include stocks (raw materials, work in progress and finished goods for resale), debtors (money owed to the business), bank balances and cash in hand.

Current assets are often described as being more 'liquid' or having higher 'liquidity', ie they are much easier to turn into cash.

What are current assets?

Assets are anything which the firm owns or has title to. Firms may have fixed assets that are long-term assets – plant, machinery and equipment, but they will also have assets that can be realised (cashed-in) in the short-term. This is generally taken, in accounting terms, to be less than a year.

The current assets are therefore ones that can be quickly realised, and change frequently. The main current assets are stock, debtors and cash.

Current Assets = Stock + Debtors + Cash

They are usually shown on the top half of the balance sheet, and the current liabilities are subtracted from them to show net current assets.

What are stocks?

Stocks are also known as inventories. They are anything that a firm has which is not currently being used for one of the firm's functions: the factory may have stocks of raw materials ready to produce; the office – stocks of stationery; and the warehouse – stocks of finished goods.

Stocks are vital to a company if it is to function smoothly. If production had to be interrupted every time the firm ran out of raw materials, the time wasted would cost the firm a lot of money. If a shop had no stock on the shelves, customers would soon desert it. The same is true of most areas in which the firm operates.

Stocks are considered to be current assets because many types of stock can be converted into cash quite readily – particularly finished goods. However, they are generally the least liquid of the current assets. At times of recession it may be very difficult for the firm to sell stocks, and so although the stocks may be listed at a certain value their true value may be lower. The other current assets are debtors and cash.

LIABILITIES

Liabilities are amounts that are owed by a business. Liabilities fall into two groups:

Long-term liabilities. These are loans that are repayable in more than one year. If the business premises were mortgaged, then that mortgage would be a long-term liability. In addition, the capital put into the business by the owner would be viewed as money that is owed by the business to the owner. This again would be a long-term liability.

Current liabilities. These are amounts which are owed by a business that must be repaid within the next 12 months. Current liabilities include money owed to creditors (for goods purchased but not yet paid for), money owed for services such as the telephone bill (often called accrued expenses), and bank overdrafts. You may think that an overdraft is repayable over a longer term but the bank can demand repayment at any time.

BALANCE SHEET

The balance sheet is one of the financial statements that organisations produce every year. It is a snapshot of the organisation's financial situation at that moment in time. It is worked out at the organisation's year end, stating the assets and liabilities at that moment.

It is given in two halves:

- the top half shows where the money is currently being used in the business (the net assets); and
- the bottom half shows where that money came from (the capital employed).

The value of the two halves must be the same: capital employed = net assets.

The money invested in the business may have been used to buy long-term assets or short-term assets. The long-term assets are known as fixed assets, and help the firm to produce.

FINAL ACCOUNTS

Examples would be machinery, equipment, computers etc, none of which actually get used up in the production process. The short-term assets are known as current assets – assets that are used day to day by the firm. The current assets may include cash, stocks and debtors.

The top half of the balance sheet will therefore be made up of the total of the fixed and current assets, less any current or long-term liabilities that the firm may have (creditors, loans and so on). It may appear as follows:

Balance Sheet of Happy Burgers Ltd, 31 December 2008

	£	£	£
Fixed Assets			
Premises			45,000
Machinery			30,000
Motor vans			19,000
			94,000
Current Assets			
Stock	23,000		
Debtors	18,000		
Bank	10,000		
Cash	2,000	53,000	
Less Current Liabilities			
Creditors		37,000	
Working Capital			16,000
			110,000
Less Long-term Liabilities			50,000
Net Assets			60,000
Financed By			
Capital	50,000		
Add Net Profit	14,000	64,000	
Less Drawings		4,000	60,000

Fixed assets are added together and the total is recorded in the third column of the balance sheet.

Current assets are added up and the total is entered in the middle column. Current liabilities are also added up and the total placed in the middle column. Current liabilities are subtracted from current assets and the resulting figure is recorded as Working Capital in the third column. If there are any long-term liabilities, they are subtracted from Fixed Assets plus Working Capital to give Net Assets.

The bottom part of the balance sheet is recorded by adding together capital and net profit and subtracting any drawings.

FINAL ACCOUNTS

CCEA SPECIMEN QUESTION - JAN 07 AS 2

Study the information below and answer the questions that follow.

Balance Sheet

Marie Debré came to Northern Ireland from France eight years ago to study at university. After graduating she worked as a sales manager for a local company and saved hard to build up the capital needed to start her own business.

She recently became aware that a small dry cleaning business, located in her neighbourhood, was being offered for sale. 'Driclean' was set up two years ago and seemed to be quite successful. As well as having premises on a busy street, it also operated a 'collect and return' service, enabling clothes to be dry cleaned without the customer having to leave home.

Marie enquired about Driclean even though she had no expertise in providing such a service. The owner provided her with financial information relating to the year ended 31st March 2006. This is shown in Table 1 below.

Table 1

Financial information relating to Driclean for the year ended 31st March

Net Profit	£3,000	Debtors	£2,000
Van	£4,000	Premises	£100,000
Cash at Bank	£3,000	Creditors	£2,000
Cleaning equipment	£10,000	Owner's Capital	£115,000
Stock	£1,000	Wages	£26,000

(a) (i) Explain the following terms:
   - Creditors
   - Owner's Capital [4]

(ii) Using appropriate information from Table 1, construct a Balance Sheet for Driclean for the year ended 31st March 2006. Clearly indicate the Working Capital of the business. [6]

(b) Discuss the usefulness of the financial information in Table 1 in helping Marie to decide whether to buy Driclean. [15]

INTERPRETING THE TRADING, PROFIT AND LOSS ACCOUNT AND BALANCE SHEET

There are many users of financial information and although the requirements of these users may differ, they all share a need for information that is easy to understand.

Generally, financial information is requested for the following reasons:

By management, who will gauge if the business is profitable and if it can pay expenses on time.

By employees, who may be interested in the firm's profitability; some staff may receive a share of company profits. They may also want to establish if management is playing by the rules and giving due regard to work councils. The 1994 EU Works Council Directive gives employees in certain multinational companies (MNCs) the right to set up works councils that must be consulted by management.

By owners, who need to ascertain if management are making good use of the business' resources.

By investors, who need to be aware of profit levels, and moreover if the level of return on their investment is comparable with other investment opportunities.

By lenders, who will judge whether the firm can make loan repayments, and how quickly these can be made. The outcome of these enquiries will determine the rate of interest charged in future dealings.

By suppliers, who will want to know if an organisation can pay its invoices on time. They will be interested in the firm's liquidity and its cash flow. Suppliers may also be interested in the business' long-term plans.

By customers, who need to be sure that the business is stable. For example, a conference organiser would need to have confidence in the business before paying over a large deposit incase the business closed before the conference took place.

By Inland Revenue and Custom and Excise, who need to ensure that the correct amounts of corporate tax and VAT are paid, based on the firm's financial figures.

By competitors, who want to establish if the firm's sales increasing or decreasing; which departments doing well; the average prices charged; and the average amount spent by customers.

Finally, all companies must send a copy of their accounts to the registrar of companies.

RATIOS

Ratios can help to measure company performance. There are four main groups of ratios: profitability, liquidity, working capital management and investment appraisal. Ratios are useful as they express financial data in simpler formats, such as percentages, and allow comparisons to be made.

Ratios can be compared to:

- the ratios of previous years in order to analyse performance
- the budget to examine if the business is performing as expected
- those of other businesses in the same industry to analyse how the firm has performed in relation to competitors.
- standards recommended by interested organisations (eg a bank)

The study of actual ratios will be covered in Unit A21.

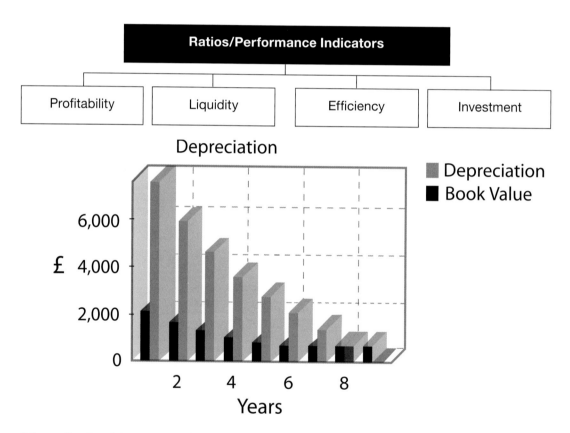

"The estimate of the amount of the fall in the value of fixed assets over a stated period of time."

Fixed assets will fall in value through time. Depending on the type of asset, this fall in value will vary from asset to asset. For example, a computer will lose value fairly quickly. It is important that this is recorded in the final accounts of the organisation to ensure that the balance sheet is a true reflection of the value of the organisation.

The cost for using a fixed asset each year is better known as depreciation. Depreciation is included with our other operating expenses in the trading/profit and loss account.

However, it is important to note that depreciation is a non-cash expense. (We never write a cheque for depreciation.)

There are different ways of calculating depreciation and each method will be appropriate to the type of fixed asset.

METHODS OF DEPRECIATION

DECLINING/REDUCING BALANCE

This method writes off a fixed percentage from the reduced balance each year. It charges most of the cost of the asset in the earlier years.

STRAIGHTLINE DEPRECIATON

Using this method, the value of the asset is reduced by a fixed amount each year. It is calculated by taking the cost of the asset and subtracting the scrap value, and dividing this figure by the estimated number of years of life of the asset. This is the most popular method of calculating depreciation.

It is important to remember that depreciation is a non-cash expense. Although we treat it as an expense in the trading/profit and loss account, no one is actually paid for this expense.

In addition to entering the annual depreciation as an expense in the trading/profit and loss account, an entry must also be made in the firm's balance sheet.

Trading/profit and loss account

Depreciation for the financial year is included in the firm's trading profit and loss account as an expense in the same way that other expenses are treated.

Balance Sheet

Two new columns are used in the Fixed Assets section of the Balance Sheet. In the first column the cost of the asset is shown. In the middle column the accumulated depreciation is entered. Accumulated depreciation (depreciation to date) is calculated by adding the 'provision for depreciation' figure from the trial balance to the depreciation estimated for the current trading period. The provision for depreciation figure that is given in the trial balance represents the depreciation that has been accounted for in previous years, but not this year's depreciation.

Depreciation to date is subtracted from the cost of the fixed asset in order to find the net book value of the assets at the end of the accounting period. These net book values are then totalled.

Fixed Assets

	Cost	Depreciation to Date	Net Book Value
Furniture	6,000	600	5,400
Motor Vans	10,000	6,000	4,000
	16,000	6,600	9,400

FINAL ACCOUNTS

One way of calculating depression is the straight line method. The following examines how this method is calculated.

Example:

Trial balance (Extract)

	Dr	Cr
	£	£
Fixed assets at cost:		
Vehicles	20,000	
Machinery	10,000	
Provision for depreciation		
Vehicles		4,000
Machinery		1,900

Note: You are to depreciate vehicles at 10% per annum using the straight line method.

The straight line method

Vehicles

The cost of the vehicles was £20,000 and we are required to depreciate them at 10% per annum using the straight line method. This method is the easiest to calculate as the depreciation charged is the same each year. Annual depreciation is a fixed percentage of the cost of the asset. In this case it is 10% of £20,000 which is £2,000 per year. This £2,000 is included in the trading/profit and loss account along with the other operating expenses.

Trading Profit and Loss Account of Happy Burgers Ltd for Year Ending 31 December 2007

	£	£	£
Sales			500,000
Less returns inwards			1,000
			499,000
Opening Stock		6,000	
Purchases	256,000		
Less returns outwards	500	255,500	
		261,500	
Less Closing Stock		10,000	
Cost of Goods Sold			251,500
Gross Profit			247,500
Add Discount received			200
			247,700
Less Expenses			

Wages and Salaries	55,000		
Add Accrual	500	55,500	
Electricity	34,000		
Less Prepaid	200	33,800	
Rent and Rates		10,000	
Discount Allowed		1,000	
Depreciation Vehicles		2,000	
Net Profit			145,400

In the balance sheet under the accumulated depreciation column, the £4,000 already provided for is added to this year's depreciation (£2,000).

Balance sheet (extract)

Fixed Assets	£	£	£
	Cost	Acc. Depreciation	NBV
Vehicles	20,000	6,000	14,000

OTHER RESOURCES

Colourpoint
Educational

Rewarding Learning

GCE Applied Business Series ———————————| AS Level ————————

ISBN: 978 1 906578 74 9
Price: £10.99
Author: Ian Bickerstaff

ISBN: 978 1 904242 73 4
Price: £10.99
Author: Eddie McKee

ISBN: 978 1 906578 01 5
Price: £15
Author: Eddie McKee

Contact Colourpoint Educational at:

Tel: 028 9182 0505 Fax: 028 9182 1900

E-mail: sales@colourpoint.co.uk

Web: www.colourpoint.co.uk

Colourpoint Books, Colourpoint House, Jubilee Business Park,
21 Jubilee Road, Newtownards, Co Down, BT23 4YH